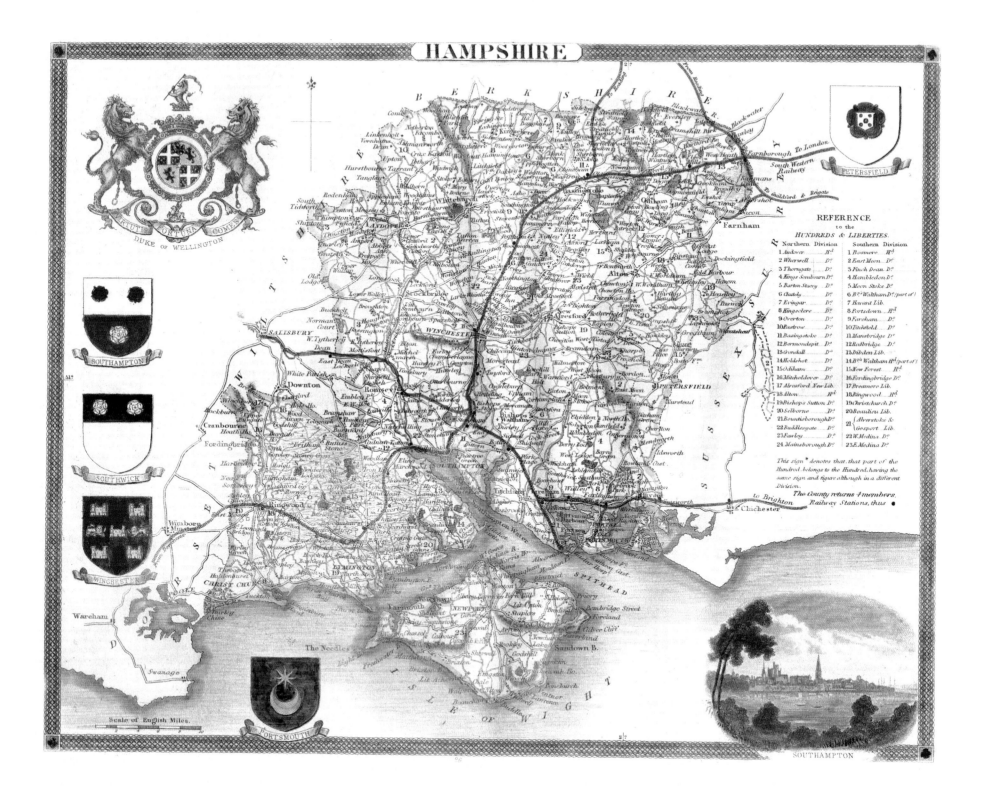

HAMPSHIRE

DUKE OF WELLINGTON

VIRTUTIS FORTUNA COMES

PETERSFIELD

SOUTHAMPTON

SOUTHWICK

WINCHESTER

PORTSMOUTH

SOUTHAMPTON

REFERENCE
to the
HUNDREDS & LIBERTIES.

Northern Division		Southern Division	
1 Andover	H.d	1 Bosmere	H.d
2 Wherwell	D.o	2 East Meon	D.o
3 Thorngate	D.o	3 Finch Dean	D.o
4 Kings Sombourn	D.o	4 Hambledon	D.o
5 Barton Stacey	D.o	5 Meon Stoke	D.o
6 Chutely	D.o	6 B.ps Waltham D.o (part of)	
7 Evingar	D.o	7 Havant Lib.	
8 Kingsclere	D.o	8 Portsdown	H.d
9 Overton	D.o	9 Fareham	D.o
10 Pastrow	D.o	10 Titchfield	D.o
11 Basingstoke	D.o	11 Mansbridge	D.o
12 Bermondspit	D.o	12 Redbridge	D.o
13 Crondall	D.o	13 Dibden Lib.	
14 Holdshot	D.o	14 B.ps Waltham H.d (part of)	
15 Odiham	D.o	15 New Forest	H.d
16 Micheldever	D.o	16 Fordingbridge	D.o
17 Alresford New Lib.		17 Breamore	D.o
18 Alton	H.d	18 Ringwood	H.d
19 Bishops Sutton	D.o	19 Christchurch	D.o
20 Selborne	D.o	20 Beaulieu Lib.	
21 Bountisborough	D.o	21 Alverstoke & Gosport Lib.	
22 Buddlesgate	D.o		
23 Fawley	D.o	22 W. Medina	D.o
24 Mainsborough	D.o	23 E. Medina	D.o

*This sign * denotes that, that part of the Hundred, belongs to the Hundred, having the same sign and figure although in a different Division.*

The County returns 4 members.

Railway Stations, thus •

Scale of English Miles.

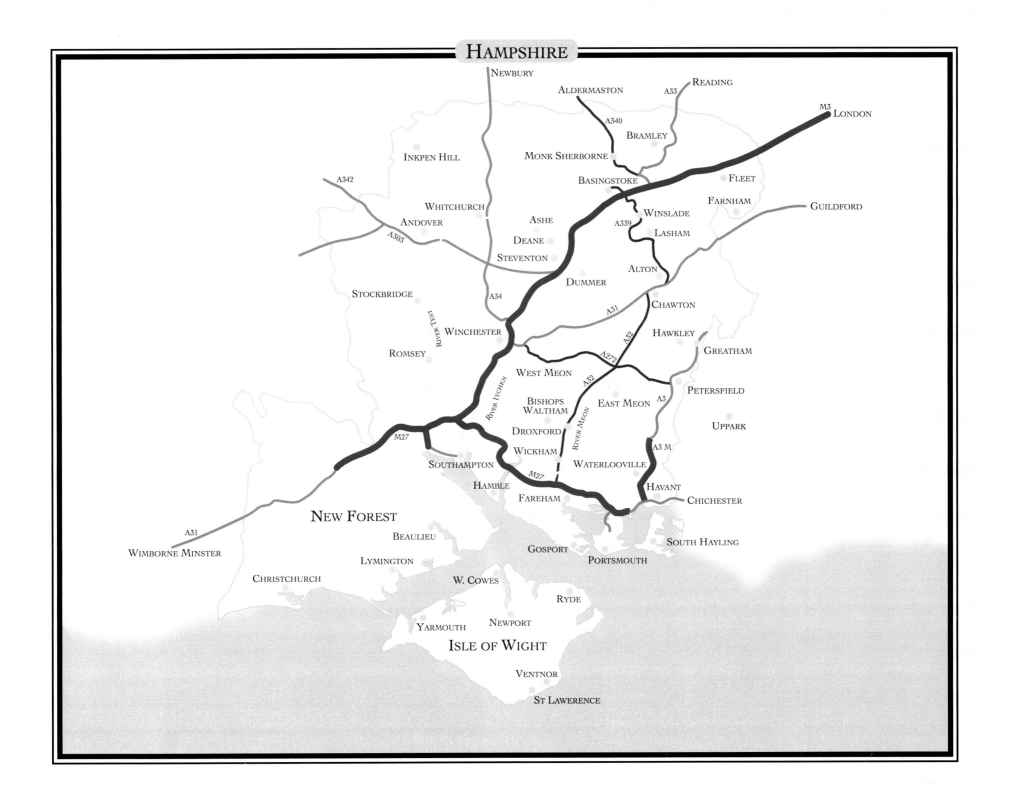

HAMPSHIRE

NEWBURY

ALDERMASTON

READING

A33

A340

BRAMLEY

M3 LONDON

INKPEN HILL

MONK SHERBORNE

BASINGSTOKE

FLEET

A342

FARNHAM

WHITCHURCH

ASHE

WINSLADE

GUILDFORD

ANDOVER

A339

LASHAM

A303

DEANE

STEVENTON

ALTON

A34

DUMMER

STOCKBRIDGE

A31

CHAWTON

A32

HAWKLEY

RIVER TEST

WINCHESTER

GREATHAM

ROMSEY

A272

RIVER ITCHEN

WEST MEON

PETERSFIELD

A32

A3

BISHOPS
WALTHAM

EAST MEON

UPPARK

M27

DROXFORD

RIVER MEON

WICKHAM

A3 M

SOUTHAMPTON

WATERLOOVILLE

HAMBLE

M27

HAVANT

FAREHAM

CHICHESTER

NEW FOREST

BEAULIEU

SOUTH HAYLING

A31

GOSPORT

WIMBORNE MINSTER

LYMINGTON

PORTSMOUTH

CHRISTCHURCH

W. COWES

RYDE

YARMOUTH

NEWPORT

ISLE OF WIGHT

VENTNOR

ST LAWERENCE

For Doris

© CHRIS BRINDLE 2012

Published by Brindle Enterprises Ltd
Ashbourne, Chapel Lane, West Bergholt, Colchester, Essex. CO6 3EG

www.ubsdell.com
mail to: brindlechris@aol.com

Chris Brindle asserts his moral right to be identified as the author of this work.
Design by Mee Mee Designs

ISBN 978-0-9573236-0-5

A CIP catalogue record for this book is available from the British Library

(Opposite: R.H.C. Ubsdell, Nelson's Monument, Portsdown Ridge circa 1841 (see page 90))

Hampshire

Discovering the 19th Century World
of
Portsmouth Artist R.H.C. Ubsdell

CHRIS BRINDLE

R.H.C. Ubsdell, Fishing Harting Pond Nov 1865
(Stacey Gardner)

Contents

Introduction

You cannot know where you are, unless you know where you've been.

My mother Doris had served as a Wren in Portsmouth during the war in the courts martial office of HMS Victory III. Her father Len had been born in Portsmouth, and her Grandfather Thomas was, according to her stories, Queen Victoria's 'Tubby Sailor'. On her death Thomas recieved a memorial tie pin from Queen Alexandra for bearing Queen Victoria's coffin onto HMY Alberta at Trinity Pier, East Cowes, following her death at Osborne. Between 1890 and 1906 Thomas served as a stoker on the second string Royal Yacht, HMY Osborne. Thomas married Leah Eleanor Ubsdell in 1890, the third and youngest daughter of Henry Ubsdell, the wayward eldest son of forgotten Portsmouth artist and photographer Richard Henry Clement Ubsdell (1812-1887). It was my search for some 200 of his pictures that lay forgotten in national collections, and unrecognised in family albums and salerooms, that led me to write this book, the story of his life, and his topographical views of Hampshire. How great an artist was Ubsdell? Well, sufficiently great that so many paintings of his survive on their merits alone, without regard to the hand of the artist that painted them. Taken together they form a remarkable history of the 19th Century, of Portsmouth, and of Hampshire.

The biggest collection of Ubsdell's paintings is held by Portsmouth Museums and Records Office (PMRS), who in 1933 acquired most of the watercolours originally painted for Sir Frederic Madden. Winchester Cathedral Library, The National Maritime Museum, The Royal Collection, and the National Trust at Uppark also have significant authenticated paintings. I acquired at auction and by private sale, two oil paintings and four watercolours, three of his carte-de-visite photographs and a number of prints from the illustrated London papers based on his watercolours and sketches, along with other identified and unidentified miniatures and works by his contemporary Hampshire artists.

My mother Doris, Wren HMS Victory III
Portsmouth 1944

Leading Petty Officer Thomas Briant recalled to service in 1914 at training establishment HMS Ganges. The smaller medal is the Coronation Medal. At the Coronation Spithead Review on 16th August 1902 each ship recieved two medals, one for a nominated officer and one for a nominated rating. Thomas recieved the rating medal.

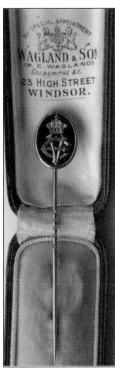

Thomas and sons, Arch; and (right) Len, Feb 1915
No717 Flight Sergeant Briant Royal Flying Corps

Tie pin presented to Thomas
by Queen Alexandra

Thomas, daughter Vi and
wife Leah Eleanor

Owners of the various images were kind enough to let me have digital copies. I plotted the topograpical locations on a map, and set out to discover Ubsdell's Hampshire; to stand where he had stood, and to record the present day version of the scene of 170 years earlier. My sat-nav took me to places no guide book ever would, past the houses of the people whose portraits he had painted, and to an understanding of the history of the county obtainable in no other way.

I decided this book had to be in full colour throughout, and Ubsdell's paintings had to dominate, but with sufficient explanation of history and geography in words to explain their significance. Historic O.S. mapping from 1910 and 1939 very beautiful in its own right, shows location, and my photographs provide comparisons, context, and adjacent sites and attractions of interest, for those who might also want to discover present day Hampshire by reference to that of Ubsdell. My book is not about recording every detail, it is about recording the most beautiful scenes, and telling as simply as possible the most significant and fascinating stories about the people who shaped Hampshire and our country. For those looking for more depth most of William Page's History of the County of Hampshire can be found at 'British History Online' and 'The Buildings of England, Hampshire and the Isle of Wight' by Nikolaus Pevsner and David Lloyd' has recently been republished in a new edition. These and other sources are acknowledged and listed in the Bibliography.

For the front cover of the book I have chosen those scenes from the past that have shown the greatest change.

CB

R.H.C. Ubsdell, Rowner
(page 60-61)

Then

R.H.C Ubsdell, Millbrook
(Vol 2 - page 24-28)

R.H.C. Ubsdell, Waterlooville
(page 130)

R.H.C. Ubsdell, Waterlooville (page 130)

R.H.C. Ubsdell,. Nelson's Monument
on Portsdown Ridge (page 90-91)

R.H.C. Ubsdell, Funtley Hill
(page 112-115)

R.H.C. Ubsdell,
Portsmouth from Southsea
Common (page 21)

R.H.C Ubsdell.
Ryde IOW from Southsea
Common (page 21)

Rowner (page 60-61)

Now

Millbrook (Vol 2 - page 24-28)

Waterlooville (page 130)

Nelson's Monument on
Portsdown Ridge (page 90-91)

Waterlooville (page 130)

Ryde IOW from Southsea
Common (page 21)

Funtley Hill (page 112-113)

Portsmouth from
Southsea Common (page 21)

21st Century Hampshire Attractions

What makes Hampshire special? What are the outstanding attractions that Ubsdell would encounter if he undertook his same journeys today? For this book I tried to find the stories behind Ubsdell's pictures, the ones I've found, and those I've yet to find or authenticate. In the process I've travelled the length and breadth of Hampshire, the IOW and bits of West Sussex. Ubsdell covered virtually all of Hampshire but Beaulieu and the New Forest are the notable exceptions. On the basis of Ubsdell's Hampshire however, here are my 'must sees' and 'must does'. They fall under four headings: Defence of the Realm; Jane Austen, Her Family & Friends; Stately Homes & Gardens; and Enjoying the Countryside, Hotels, Eating and Drinking:-

DEFENCE OF THE REALM

2

3

4

Portsmouth Harbour had paramount strategic importance, as will be appreciated by a visit to the Historic Dockyard (see pages 38-41). Here, in the oldest part of the still active Naval Dockyard, you can explore (1) Nelson's flagship HMS Victory, (2) the iron hulled HMS Warrior, and Henry VIII's Mary Rose. As part of your ticket you can take the harbour tour, and see the ships of the current Royal Navy at anchor, (3) e.g. (HMS Illustrious & Mounts Bay alongside Basin No1 Royal Naval Dockyard). As part of your ticket you can take the water-bus across to the military exhibits on the Gosport side. There is the excellent 'Explosion! Museum of Naval Firepower', at the old gunpowder magazine and munitions facility at (4) Priddy's Hard, and the (5) Royal Navy Submarine Museum, in part of the old submarine base of HMS Dolphin.

To defend Portsmouth from attack, Portsea (where the dockyard is), Portsmouth Town (where the army barracks were, together with Ubsdell's High Street, and the sailor's haunts on 'Spice Island'), and Gosport (where the provisioning of the navy was done) were all walled and fortified towns, and evidence of their defences remain.

5

Defences include, The Ramparts (see pages 32-37), Southsea Castle, and (6) the Historic Gunwharf Quay (which dealt with the cannons and artillery) now transformed into a shopping, eating and entertainment experience. The Palmerston Forts are magnificent. You can visit (7) Fort Nelson which is part of the Royal Armouries, and tells the story of all types of artillery through the ages, and go horse riding at Fort Widley. (see pages 90 – 91). (8) Fort Brockhurst on Gosport is also open to the public at restricted times.

Hampshire County Council publishes an excellent 'Defence of the Realm' leaflet with money saving vouchers for these and many other similar attractions in the County.

JANE AUSTEN: HER FAMILY & FRIENDS

Jane's writing was founded on her youthful experiences when living at Steventon in the Upper Test Valley (Vol 2 - pages 64-77) as modified by holidays and visits to family and friends, and more difficult times whilst living in Bath and Southampton (Vol 2 - page 16). Her later writing and the revision of her work for publication was mostly done at Chawton Cottage near Alton, which lies at the head of the most wonderful piece of Hampshire countryside, 'Petersfield and the Beech Hangers' (Vol 2 - pages 80-117). The main Austen places of interest are: The site of Steventon Rectory (foreground) and (1) new Rectory (background), (2) Steventon Church, (3) Chawton Cottage Museum, (4) Chawton Church (rebuilt 1872/3), (5) Chawton Great House, (6) the rebuilt church at Deane, (7) Ashe rectory where she danced and the rebuilt Ashe church, and Winchester for the cathedral where she is buried and (8) the house at 8 College Street where she died.

Hampshire (and I include Ubsdell's bits of the IOW and West Sessex) has some wonderful Homes and Gardens that are open to the public. Top of the list has to be (1) Mottisfont Abbey (Vol 2 - pages 21-23) for its wonderful position in the Test Valley, its tea room, its walled garden, its art exhibitions on the top floor, and the sheer puzzle of working out what was built when! Next on the list is (2) Hinton Ampner (page 127) for its wonderful gardens and views. (3) The Vyne for its historical connections (Vol 2 - page 132). (4) Appuldurcombe near Godshill IOW overlooking Wroxall, for its connection with the Earl of Yarborough (see pages 86-89) and (5) The Grange (Vol 2 - page 36), for the sheer romance of its position, and (6) Gilbert White's House at Selborne (Vol 2 - pages 112-114) as much for the garden as anything else, and to soak up White's love of The Hangers.

1

2

3 *(National Trust)*

4

5

6

Driving and walking round Hampshire I found some places I was particularly fond of. In first place came the Hampshire restaurant of chef Atul Kochhar, 'the king of spices', (1) Vatika (now unfortunately looking for a new location). The restaurant has now re-opened under head chef Paul Dive formerly with Ramond Blanc at Le Manoir aux Quat'saisons. It is next to the wonderful (2) Wickham Vineyard. Next is (3) The Hawkley Inn because you can just get up in the morning and walk out of its door straight into the stunning Hanger scenery, (4) is the excellent food in the eccentric surroundings of The Thomas Lord in West Meon. (5) is the excellent place to stay and eat in Lymington, The Stanwell House Hotel, (6) is the The White Lion a friendly place to stay and eat in Wherwell, (7) is the Coach & Horses at Compton an excellent place to drink beer in the afternoon and play bar billiards. Fine for sleeping and eating is (8) The Trooper Inn near Froxfield on the Steep to Ropley road, and the Red Lion (9) at Chalton which has a wonderful terrace on which to take refreshments on a sunny day. My favourite hotel in Portsmouth is (10) the Queens. (11) The Crab and Lobster has an interesting history in Ventnor and (12) The Olde George is a good place to stay in East Meon.

1

2

3

4

5

6

7

8

9

10

11

12

Finally I must give a special mention to the City Museum Portsmouth whose various Permanent and Special exhibitions are well worth paying a visit; and the Portsmouth History Centre in the Central Library, as a good place to research Ubsdell and other local history subjects.

Hampshire has some wonderful cycle paths and long distance footpaths. Those that come closest to Ubsdell's churches are the following:-

The main cycle paths on old railway routes are indicated on the map opposite. These are wonderful opportunities to take exercise as strenuous as you make it, mostly in beautiful countryside, free from pollution and traffic hazards.

The Test Valley Cycle Path (3) – Stoneymarsh to Cottonworth
Meon Valley Cycle Path (5) – Wickham to West Meon
Hayling Billy Cycle Path (7) – West side of Hayling Island
IOW Railway Cycle paths – Newport to Sandown
Newport to Cowes
Wooton to Newport
Brading to Bembridge

GOSPORT CYCLE PATHS
Gosport to Fareham northern section shared with express buses
Gosport to Stokes Bay

NORTH – SOUTH LONG DISTANCE FOOTPATHS
(marked on map opposite)

TEST WAY (2) 44 miles – Inkpen Hill – Linkenholt – Hurstbourne Tarrant – Stoke – St. Mary Bourne – Longparish – Chilbolton – Mayfly P.H. – Stockbridge – King's Somborne – Romsey – Broadlands – Eling Tide Mill.

WAYFARER'S WALK (1) – 70 miles – Inkpen Beacon – Burghclere – North Oakley – Deane, Dummer – Brown Candover – New Alresford – Cheriton – Droxford – Hambledon – Denmead – Bedhampton – Emsworth (near Portsmouth)

HANGERS WAY (4) – 21 miles – Alton Railway Station – east Worldham – Selborne – Noar Hill – Hawkley – Steep – Petersfield – Buriton – Queen Elizabeth County Park

MEON VALLEY PILGRIMAGE TRAIL – Variants on the Meon Valley

Cycle Path Route – a booklet price £4 is available in most of the Meon Valley churches.

If cycling the Meon Valley Trail in one direction West Meon is a good place to start, as the prevailing gradient is downhill. Walkers can fairly easily scramble up at most road over-bridges but leaving the trail with a bike for the non-athletic is less easy at overbridges after Droxford. Droxford is a good place for a rest and the old railway hotel now called 'The Hurdles' is recommended. In June 1944 Allied leaders including, Churchill, Eisenhower and de Gaulle met in a train carriage at Droxford station to discuss the imminent D-Day invasion. See Bibliography (p145) for on-line guides to the cyclepath.

STAUNTON WAY (6) – 8.5 miles Havant – Rowlands Castle – Chalton – Queen Elizabeth Country Park to join with the South Downs Way.

EAST – WEST DIAGONAL LONG DISTANCE FOOTPATHS

THE SOUTH DOWNS WAY – Eastbourne to Lewes to Devil's Dyke to Steyning to Amberley – South Harting – Buriton – Queen Elizabeth Country Park – Butser Hill – HMS Mercury – East Meon – Warnford – Cheriton – Winchester

THE KING'S WAY – Portchester Castle – Nelson's Monument, Fort Nelson – World's End – Soberton – Bishop's Waltham – Upham – Cheesefoot Head – Ovington – Part of the Itchen Way (that follows the river from source near Hinton Ampner to its estuary at Woolston) – Avington – Nun's Walk – Winchester King Alfred's statue

PILGRIMS' WAY – Mont St Michel (France) Portsmouth (Ferry Port) – Coastal path – Wymering – Portsdown Ridge – Southwick – North Boarhunt – Mislingford – Swanmore – Bishop's Waltham – with the King's way on the Roman Road to Upham – then with the Monarch's Way to Owlesbury – Twyford – St. Cross – Winchester

MONARCH'S WAY – Worcester to Shoreham – includes a section in the reverse direction – Rowlands Castle – Blendworth – Horndean – near Hambledon – Broadhalfpenny Down – Bat & Ball – Old Winchester Hill – South Downs Way – Warnford – Upham – Pilgrims Trail.

HAMPSHIRE:- FOOTPATHS AND OLD RAILWAY CYCLEPATHS

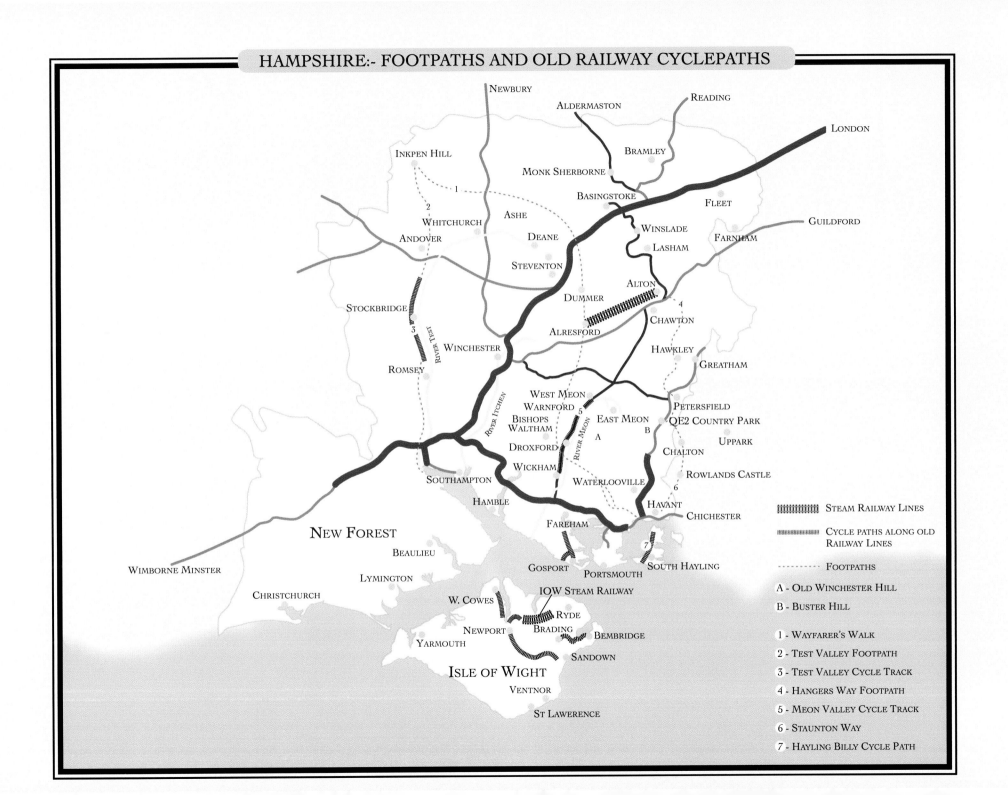

NEWBURY
ALDERMASTON
READING
LONDON
INKPEN HILL
BRAMLEY
MONK SHERBORNE
1
BASINGSTOKE
FLEET
2
WHITCHURCH
ASHE
WINSLADE
ANDOVER
DEANE
LASHAM
FARNHAM
GUILDFORD
STEVENTON
ALTON
DUMMER
4
STOCKBRIDGE
CHAWTON
3
ALRESFORD
HAWKLEY
RIVER TEST
WINCHESTER
GREATHAM
ROMSEY
RIVER ITCHEN
WEST MEON
PETERSFIELD
WARNFORD
5
QE2 COUNTRY PARK
BISHOPS WALTHAM
EAST MEON
B
UPPARK
RIVER MEON
A
DROXFORD
CHALTON
WICKHAM
ROWLANDS CASTLE
WATERLOOVILLE
6
SOUTHAMPTON
HAVANT
HAMBLE
CHICHESTER
FAREHAM
NEW FOREST
7
BEAULIEU
WIMBORNE MINSTER
GOSPORT
SOUTH HAYLING
LYMINGTON
PORTSMOUTH
CHRISTCHURCH
IOW STEAM RAILWAY
W. COWES
RYDE
NEWPORT
BRADING
BEMBRIDGE
YARMOUTH
SANDOWN
ISLE OF WIGHT
VENTNOR
ST LAWERENCE

|||||||||| STEAM RAILWAY LINES

▬▬▬▬ CYCLE PATHS ALONG OLD RAILWAY LINES

- - - - FOOTPATHS

A - OLD WINCHESTER HILL
B - BUSTER HILL

1 - WAYFARER'S WALK
2 - TEST VALLEY FOOTPATH
3 - TEST VALLEY CYCLE TRACK
4 - HANGERS WAY FOOTPATH
5 - MEON VALLEY CYCLE TRACK
6 - STAUNTON WAY
7 - HAYLING BILLY CYCLE PATH

R.H.C. Ubsdell, Richard Henry Clement Ubsdell Self Portrait 1837

Portsmouth and the Story of the Watercolours

By 1839 the family of Richard Henry Clement Ubsdell was beginning to starve.

The Whig government had been in power since 1830, and by the maintenance of the Corn Laws had protected the incomes of the big landowners by raising levies on imported corn, but in so doing kept the price of bread high for ordinary people. Local Enclosure Acts continued to be passed whereby the strips of land that had characterised the mediaeval system of ownership were re-parcelled into consolidated holdings, to the advantage of the larger landowners, forcing many people off the land and into the emerging industrialised cities. The population was expanding, and the increasing mechanisation of agriculture was driving rural wages down. The resulting dissent was being vigorously suppressed. The Reform Act of 1832 had improved the electoral system, and Ubsdell paying a rent of £20 per annum on his house at 135 High Street Portsmouth would now qualify for a vote, but would otherwise have had little power to affect the events that were happening round him. These were the causes of the Chartist movement in England, and discontent throughout Western Europe, that would grow throughout the 1840s, leading to a new wave of revolution.

There had been peace with France, Britain's most serious rival, since Napoleon had been finally defeated in 1815 and the rest of Western Europe was fragmented and could be held in balance by political, rather than military means.

The Royal Navy had been reduced in strength, and shipbuilding and repair, Portsmouth's major industry, was at a low ebb, and its resurgence to meet the growing threat of France had yet to happen. The Royal Navy experimented with steam ships, iron hulls, breech loading cannon, rotating turrets and explosive shells, but naval architecture had yet to find a single direction, and wooden sided ships powered by sail still dominated the Naval fleet.

Richard's daughter, Mary Lavinia was born and joined Richard's family of wife Mary, and sons Henry, George and Thomas, and was baptised on the 12th August 1840. Richard had a small house on the main Portsmouth thoroughfare, at 135 High Street opposite the theatre. It was here in the front room he maintained his studio and small art gallery, keeping up the appearance of gentility on a very low income.

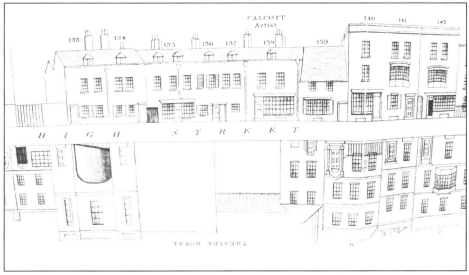

Ubsdell's first house & studio 135, High Street, Portsmouth (PMRS)
Charpentier's Stranger's Guide to Portsmouth, 1842

This was particularly hard to do in early Victorian times because there were no cheap imported goods, and everything including fuel, and all but the cheapest food, was expensive relative to the wages of the labouring classes.

In an age before cameras, photocopiers, postcards and colour printing Ubsdell's initial income came from copying documents maps and pictures, and commissions from amateur historians Julian & Henry Slight. He hand coloured monochrome prints, sold simple watercolours of Portsmouth scenes, and painted miniature watercolour portraits of people on small rectangles of very thin ivory. Throughout his career he was conscious of trying to earn a living daily wage, and therefore tailored the amount of time he put into a painting to suit the pocket of the likely purchaser. In judging the 'quality' of Ubsdell's work this has to be borne in mind. His best portraits and subject paintings stand comparison with the finest of the age, but all his works *combined* make a remarkable record of Hampshire in early and mid Victorian times.

This book is a collection of Ubsdell's surviving watercolour topographical views of Portsmouth, the Isle of Wight & Hampshire. It includes his earliest known work, the 'Old Gaol on the High Street' from 1830, and from around the same time, Owen Tottyer's House on Lombard Street where the great plague started. Also included is a simple watercolour of Southsea Common and a very early oil painting of the Town Hall that stood in the middle of the High Street until 1836. Also early is the view of the Isle of Wight seen from Southsea Common.

Artists without private means need patrons, and in Ubsdell's case his early days were sustained by the Slight brothers, and in the late 1830s by John Deane. John Deane, with his brother Charles invented the diving helmet and used it to salvage a large number of wrecks including the 'Mary Rose' and the 'Royal George' both wrecked off Portsmouth. John commissioned Ubsdell to record many of his finds as an aid to selling the recoveries to collectors, and to create the artwork for his 'cabinet', a collection of prints detailing the invention of the diving helmet, and recording the objects recovered. Between 1836 and 1840 Ubsdell had recorded the individual objects and then worked to combine the individual illustrations into completed spreads ready for reproduction. In the end however the expense of having lithographs created from the watercolours, and then having the lithographs hand coloured to match the beauty of Ubsdell's original watercolours defeated the enterprise, and Ubsdell therefore required a new patron.

R.H.C. Ubsdell, Old Gaol on the High Street, 1830
(PMRS 1946/106)

R.H.C. Ubsdell, Owen Tottyer's House where the great plague started
(PMRS 1946/105)

R.H.C. Ubsdell, Southsea Common, the old Semaphore Telegraph and Portsmouth in the background, the Magazine and the Cricketers Public House in the foreground. (PMRS 1945/419/56)

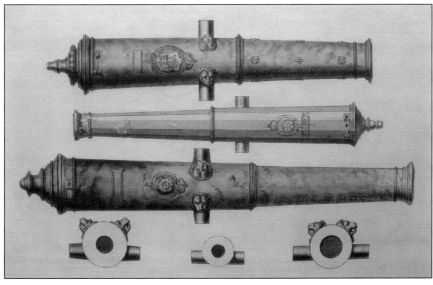

R.H.C. Ubsdell, Hand coloured lithograph outline of guns recovered from the wreck of the Mary Rose in 1836. (PMRS 1967/679/2)

Ubsdell found that recording historic subjects was a useful theme to pursue, and by their very nature churches encapsulate history, making them of very considerable interest to antiquarians and collectors of historic images. Ubsdell would probably have seen a very fine watercolour of Hambledon Church painted by his rival Richard Poate in 1836, and would have recognised in churches, images that could usefully be added to the pictures on show in his gallery. Ubsdell's distant ancestors were of noble blood, but he himself was the son of a waiter in a Portsmouth inn, and had only a basic education. The study of history was therefore a way for him of gaining more of an equality with his potential patrons, although he could never make up for his lack of education in the classics of Greek and Latin.

Portsmouth had three ancient churches all controlled by the Augustinian Priory of Southwick. The earliest church in Portsmouth was St Mary's situated on high land a mile away from the sea, the origins of which date back to 1170 when it was founded by Baldwin de Portsea. By 1838 Ubsdell was probably fascinated enough by ancient churches to have his son Thomas baptised there, and it was probably one of the first church exteriors and interiors he recorded in watercolours. The original church survived until 1843 although its tower was incorporated in its successor, by Portsmouth architect Thomas Ellis Owen but that was only to last until Sir Arthur Blomfield's grand church completed between 1887 and 1889.

R.H.C. Ubsdell, Town Hall in the middle of the High Street 1830 pulled down 1836. (PMRS 1946/63)

Ubsdell's other children were baptised at St. Thomas à Becket the successor to a chapel founded c.1187 by local mercantile shipping magnate John de Gisors, and built in Caen and Binstead stone. This was just off the High Street in Portsmouth and would, in the 20th century, become Portsmouth Cathedral. Like St Mary's, St Thomas's was also under the auspices of Southwick Priory, the remains of which Ubsdell would also record. Ubsdell completed a watercolour of the interior of St. Thomas's church from which lithographic prints were made at around the time of his marriage in 1833.

R.H.C. Ubsdell, St Thomas à Becket Interior
(CHU2/5V/23)

R.H.C. Ubsdell, St Mary's Kingston Interior before 1843
(PMRS 1960/91)

R.H.C. Ubsdell, St Mary's Kingston Before 1843 South Side
(PMRS 1945/721)

R.H.C. Ubsdell, St Mary's Kingston North Side before 1843
(PMRS 1945/719)

R.H.C. Ubsdell, St Mary's Kingston South Side 1843 - 1887
(PMRS 1960/91)

R.H.C. Ubsdell, St Mary's Kingston North Side 1889 to date

The last church controlled by Southwick Priory was the chapel of the Domus Dei erected in 1214. The Domus Dei (God's House) was a walled semi-monastic village covering two and a half acres. It had six brethren and six sisters supervised by a warden, and housed travellers, and sick and elderly people. The beautiful chapel and the adjacent infirmary hall (roofless since 1941) survive. Much of the rest of the village was swept

Winchfield in the far North East of Hampshire or to Southampton. He would carry sketch books ruler and pencils, and some simple watercolours, and try and obtain work and shelter as he went. He would call at the country houses and inns and sketch and try and get commissions for miniatures, from servants and masters alike, taking shelter where he could. Many of these had sufficient merit to be

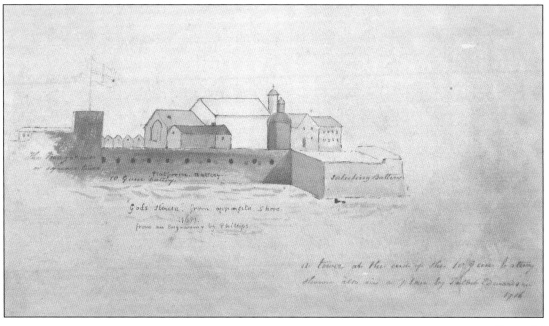

Domus Dei
(PMRS 857A)

away when the fortifications of Portsmouth were built in the 17th Century. Ubsdell made a copy of a drawing of the original Domus Dei, and incorporated the Chapel, by then used by the Garrison, into his magnificent watercolour of Governor's Green painted in 1860.

Many artists were peripatetic. If the work would not come to you, you could go to the work; and so in the summer months Ubsdell began to travel across Hampshire. He would probably walk, although as he ranged further afield he may have begun to ride a horse, and finally in the mid 1840s he may have taken the London & South Western railway to

preserved, rather than discarded by subsequent generations. The portraits of the gentry survive with the name of the ancestor vaguely remembered, but with the name of the painter lost, and considered irrelevant. Many miniatures probably by Ubsdell come up at auction, but go unrecognised. He appears not to have signed his portraits, relying on a label on the frame or case so the attribution gets lost as canvasses are relined (backed by a new canvas) or reframed, and as miniatures are removed from their presentation cases and framed.

R.H.C. Ubsdell, Titchfield 1840
(PMRS 1945/419/61)

Ubsdell's perambulations took him from one church to another, for in sketching the tombs at Titchfield Church in September 1839 he acquired a new patron, Sir Frederic Madden, who was intent on the same quest of inspecting the tombs. A sequence of correspondence began that is now in the Record Office at Portsmouth.

Madden had been born in Portsmouth in 1801 and for 29 years until his retirement in 1866, was Keeper of the Department of Manuscripts at the British Museum. A skilled antiquarian and linguist, he collected a vast personal collection of historical documents. His never to be fulfilled intention was to write a history of Portsmouth and Hampshire. Ubsdell hoped that his works might illustrate such a work, a hope unfulfilled until now, some two hundred years after his birth.

Madden died in 1873 a bitter and frustrated man. He had been passed over for the Principal's job at the British Museum, and consequently his personal collection was auctioned at his death, rather than being left to the Nation. Ubsdell's watercolours remained together as a collection in private hands and were acquired by Portsmouth Record Office in 1933. The collection was fortunate to spend the war time years in the Portsmouth vaults, and therefore escaped the fate of many of Ubsdell's framed works, on the walls of the old Museum and the new Guildhall that were both destroyed by German bombing.

Ubsdell spent much of 1840 in correspondence with Madden in respect of subjects he might like added to his collection, and eventually in October 1840 he sent him a package containing 21 items and a bill for £8 18s 0d. Included were the inscriptions on the Wryotheslye tomb at Tichfield and copies of all the inscriptions and heraldic shields, a version of the White House that contained the jail, a version of the Telegraph on Southsea Common, the north side of Charles Fort on Gosport and Ubsdell's first exterior view of a church for Madden:- Titchfield. Madden is characteristically taken aback by the bill and requests that Ubsdell does not make any more copies for him.

Ubsdell, however, is convinced that Madden will buy more pictures of churches, and they might well sell if exhibited back at his studio and art gallery. If not, possibly the Bishop of Winchester might be interested. The Vicar of Portsmouth, the Reverend Charles Henville had seen Ubsdell's watercolours of churches and knowing the Bishop to be a collector of such things, had made a suitable introduction. The Bishop asked for a portfolio of churches to be sent to him at Farnham Castle during the first week of November 1841.

Sir Frederic Madden
(Hampshire Records Office 15/M84/P1 folio 30)

Ubsdell's summer campaign of 1841 started with South Hayling, on Hayling Island on the 13th July, apparently painting both Chalton and Southwick St Peter on July 18th, Farlington on 20th July, Fareham on the 27th, Hamble-le-Rice on the 30th, with Catherington, Fareham and Bishops Waltham, also being finished in that month. Alverstoke and Rowner were also completed that Summer.

August saw Ubsdell in the Meon Valley; Wickham, Droxford, and Meonstoke all being apparently painted on August 3rd, with Exton being seen on the 5th, and with Warnford, West Meon & Hound also being covered that month. The end of August saw a tour of the Isle of Wight and the painting of Northwood, which is just south of West Cowes.

R.H.C. Ubsdell, Charles Fort, Gosport 1840
(PMRS 1945/419/27)

In August 1841 Ubsdell parcelled up watercolours of Bursledon, Meonstoke, Blendworth, Hound, Wickham, Rowner, Wickham North Front, Southwick, 'Wymmering', South Hayling, Droxford, Crofton, Boarhunt, Exton, Charlton, Farlington, Hambledon, Clanfield, Waterlooville, Warnford, Hamble Le Rice, Fareham, Widley, West Meon, Corhampton, Bishops Waltham, Catherington, Shirrell Heath and Funtley, and presented Madden with a bill for £11 7s 6d.

1842 saw a watercolour of Durley on January 3rd. Ubsdell parcelled up the remaining work from the previous year including Alverstoke, Bedhampton, Havant, Warblington, and a historic view of Gosport, and sent them off to Madden on 7th January 1842. '.....having been very ill during the past half year I find myself a little behind and being obliged to pay £15 to Reeves & Son of Cheapside London on the 12th. I was in hope that these drawings being so well finished may be the manner of your

trying to take shelter from huge grey storm clouds.

Ubsdell had successfully started to sell pictures to the Bishop, and the first two were probably a copy of Warnford and the starkly modern, newly opened Sarisbury Green.

1842 however saw Ubsdell's fortunes change for the better. Queen Victoria was at Brighton planning to tour the South Coast and she was to visit Portsmouth on March 21st. Ubsdell had been chosen to produce the illuminated address to be given to the Queen, and to record the meeting of Queen Victoria & Portsmouth Corporation. He went to London to record the images of the Queen's Chief ministers. Ubsdell was at Court when Franz Xaver Winterhalter was painting the English Royal Family for the first time. Probably with the assistance of Winterhalter Ubsdell also gained access to the French Court, and although Queen Victoria probably never sat for him, the French King did, thus justifying Ubsdell's claim that

R.H.C. Ubsdell, Wymering 1842
(PMRS 1945/419/77)

R.H.C. Ubsdell, Warnford, version for the
Bishop of Winchester 1841
(The Dean and Chapter of Winchester Cathedral)

R.H.C. Ubsdell, Sarisbury Green 1841
(The Dean and Chapter of Winchester Cathedral)

extending your kind aid'. Madden rejected two watercolours of Newport IOW and a historical view of Alverstoke, and after criticising the architectural details of the pictures and requesting that Ubsdell send no more pictures, Madden remitted £12 17s 6d. Ubsdell had not mentioned that during the illness which had presumably hit the whole family, his one year old daughter Mary Lavinia Ubsdell had died of pneumonia 2 days before Christmas. The average cost of the watercolours was 7s 6d each. There is one very 'dark' picture completed around this time a landscape of Wymering, a hugely atmospheric picture of a figure in the foreground

he was 'Miniature Painter To The King 1842'. Whilst in France, Ubsdell probably participated in a proposed artistic project to decorate public buildings on both sides of the Channel to commemorate the Queen's first visit abroad, to the Château d'Eu in Normandy in 1843. A work at the Château attributed to an unlikely named artist called Hippolyte Adrien Démétrius Provost-Dumarchais bears many elements in Ubsdell's style! It would appear he chose a similar scheme to decorate the side walls of Portchester Castle theatre eight years later.

Little topographical work was therefore completed in 1842/3.

R.H.C. Ubsdell, Crab and Lobster Inn, Ventnor IOW 1843
(PMRS 1943/419/62)

The notable exception being the watercolour of the Crab & Lobster Inn at Ventnor on the Isle of Wight, doubtless the venue for a family holiday in 1843. It was probably on this holiday that Ubsdell sketched the interior of St Lawrence Church and the idea formed in his mind that he would use his preliminary drawings of his portrait miniatures, to create a composite picture of the famous people he had met in the past two years, all sat round listening to a sermon in reputedly the smallest church in England.

The Bishop of Winchester, Charles Richard Sumner, was to provide the impetus for a further bout of church painting in 1845, and watercolours of West Cowes, Millbrook, East Wellow, East Tytherley, Ashley, Upper Clatford, Hartley Wintney and Liss were all completed this year.

Aware that he might have two customers for the same image Ubsdell ensured that he kept a tracing of the pictures, should he find he could make a second sale. He made a catalogue of available images, an idea he was to come back to in the late 1850s when with the advent of photography, his Portsmouth Stereoscopic Company was to create a library kept on glass negatives, of stereoscopic images of Portsmouth and the Isle of Wight.

After a gap of some two years Ubsdell recommenced his correspondence with Madden, on 7th October 1845 informing him that houses between the Sally Port and Point were to be pulled down, and offering to make a sketch of them. Madden responded commissioning him to make a drawing of his late father's house in St Thomas's Street.

1846 was the final year of the church watercolours. Southwick Priory, Millbrook, Wherwell, Whitchurch, Overton, Foxcott Chapel, Monk Sherborne, and Bramley painted in 1845 were to find their way to Madden together with Petersfield, Steep, Colemore, Newton Valence, East Tisted, Selborne, Priors Dean, East Worldham, Alton, Shalden, Herriard, Winslade, and Silchester.

In 1846 the Bishop took Lasham, Greatham, and similar versions to Madden of East Tisted, Hartley Mauditt, and West Worldham; and an interestingly different version of Millbrook.

No	NAME	REFERENCE
1	Earl of Yarborough	Named on back of canvas, founder member of The Royal Yacht Squadron, Cowes Castle, IOW.
2	Lady Emma Lascelles, Baroness Portman	Lady of the Bedchamber to Queen Victoria (1827 – 1851) involved in the "Scandal of The Bedchamber 1839"
3	Charles Cecil Cope Jenkinson 3rd Earl of Liverpool	(Country Seat, Buxted Park, Uckfield) Younger half brother of the Robert Jenkinson the 2nd Earl of Liverpool Succeeded to the title 1828. Had served as Under Secretary of State for War and the Colonies 1809 -10, 1841-1846 Lord Steward of the Queen's Household in the Tory government of Sir Robert Peel. Daughters, Catherine, Selina, Louisa, were all amateur painters represented in the Royal Collection.
4	Archdeacon Samuel Wilberforce	Son of William Wilberforce, Chaplain to Queen Victoria at Osborne, Succeeded his Cousin Charles Richard Sumner in 1869 as Bishop of Winchester, Debated against Huxley in the Oxford Union, opposing Charles Darwin's Theory of Evolution.
5	Charles Yorke, 4th Earl of Hardwicke	(Country Seat, Wimpole Hall, Cambridgeshire) Succeeded to the title 18/11/1834 a Lord in Waiting to Queen Victoria 1841-46 resigning to oppose the repeal of the Corn Laws. Entered Royal Naval College Portsmouth in Feb 1813 at a time when life-long friend John Christian Schetky served as drawing master (1811-1836) Extensive Naval Career, and member of Royal Yacht Squadron.
6	John Howard	Portsmouth Town Clerk
7	Alderman Charles Robbins	Draper & Long standing Portsmouth Alderman, lived at Mile End Villa in the Commercial Rd.
8	Charles Richard Sumner	(caricature) Bishop of Winchester, dressed as a shepherd, leaning on his crook, closely observing his cousin and protégé Archdeacon Samuel Wilberforce. A patron of Ubsdell's from Nov 1841
9	Sir Frederic Madden (caricature)	Born Portsmouth, Keeper of Manuscripts at the British Museum A patron of Ubsdell from 1840 Sumner is shown as a shepherd and Madden is seen in a stylised sheep pen.
10	Prince Louis-Philippe Albert d'Orleans	(24/8/1838-8/9/1894) son of Prince Ferdinand-Philippe (d1842) grandson of Louis Philippe, King of the French, and heir to the French Throne.
11	The Duchess D'Orleans	The widow of Prince Ferdinand-Philippe and the mother of Prince Louis-Philippe Albert
12	Richard Henry Clement Ubsdell	The artist placed just underneath the vanishing point of the lines of perspective
13	Mary Ann Ubsdell nee Pennal	Sitting next to the artist, also seen looking out a top floor window in Ubsdell's painting "Governor's Green"
14	Mary Lavinia Ubsdell	Daughter of the artist baptized 12th August 1839 died of pneumonia 23rd December 1841
15	The Font	Presumably symbolising the short life of Mary Lavinia
16	Prince Albert Edward, Prince of Wales	Is central in the picture looking forward, so presumably of greatest importance.
17	Possibly Prince Albert	The full face possibly taken from the Winterhalter painting of 1842
18	Possibly Queen Victoria	Possibly the Winterhalter face of 1842 looking straight forward and placed in a bonnet
19	Possibly William Chinn Ubsdell	From the position next to the Ubsdell group, the most probable possibility
20	Possibly John Portal	Known to have been painted in 1846, but also possibly earlier?
21	Jane Anna Elizabeth Lefroy née Austen	Anna Lefroy niece of Jane Austen first child of James Austen, Jane Austen's eldest brother

Left: R.H.C. Ubsdell, Sermon at St Lawrence Church, Ventnor IOW. April 1844.
Comprised of images of the famous people Ubsdell had painted as miniatures.

July 22. 1847. ABOLITION of FREE MART FAIR.

THE LAST FREE MART FAIR 1847

The Free Mart Fair ran annually from 10th July until the 24th. Its commencement would be signified by the display, from a public building, of a wooden representation of a gloved hand representing justice and friendship. At the end of proceedings it would be taken down. Ubsdell shows the hand displayed on the front wall of the old jail in his painting on page (x). When the fair ended many of the stalls would set up again on the spectacular setting of the Portsdown Ridge. On a good year the fair would run the length of the High Street with the larger attractions taking up positions on Grand Parade, and some of the more dubious attractions on vacant plots of private land.

The Fair included all manner of goods for sale but its main emphasis was entertainment. There were human freak shows, and in the days before zoos were common, animal circuses and menageries. There were waxworks and theatre companies performing all manner of plays and re-enactments.

It was the 'Vauxhalls' however, named after the notorious Vauxhall Pleasure Gardens on the South bank of the Thames, that would bring about the demise of the Free Mart Fair. The Vauxhalls offering music, dancing, drinking, and women until dawn, were increasingly castigated as Victorian values took over from those of the free living Georgians. The end finally came in 1847.

Ubsdell's watercolour shows the scene in Grand Parade viewed from the High Street. Big booths dominate the area. In the background there is a menagerie and along the right of the picture possibly circus acts, and two competing Vauxhalls. In the foreground there is a Punch and Judy show, rifle shooting, games of chance, and a boy climbing a lamppost to get a better view.

In the left of the picture there is a stall selling childrens' toys. The notice announcing the end of the fair, and the severe punishments promised to anyone trying to revive it, hangs on the stall side, together with an advertisement for a Vauxhall situated a short distance away. There are dolls and toy soldiers, and a model of the Royal Yacht Victoria & Albert 1, a paddle steamer launched at Pembroke on 1 July 1843. Hanging down the right hand side of the booth is a model train. The

Left: R.H.C. Ubsdell, Abolition of The Free Mart Fair 1847
(PMRS 1995/791)

Grand Parade

railway line to Portsmouth via Brighton had reached Portsmouth Town station on the 14 June 1847. The line from Southampton to Portsmouth would open on 1 October of the following year, and the direct line via Guildford and Godalming on 24 January 1859. It was not till 1876 however that the Military Authorities permitted a railway to breach Portsmouth's fortifications, allowing the extension to Portsmouth Harbour to be built.

The painting has an interesting history. It had been in the (1836) Town Hall in the High Street that became the town's museum when the 1890 Guildhall was built. Many of Ubsdell's paintings were on display there and were destroyed in the war by German bombing. However this painting was 'rescued' from the ruins and found its way onto the walls of the Dolphin pub in the High Street. During research for a book on the fair published by Portsmouth City Council the painting was identified and the pub landlords graciously returned the painting to the City collection.

Portraits were to dominate Ubsdell's future output. However there were exceptions. Governor's Green is a huge watercolour consisting of 3 separate sheets mounted on linen and fixed to a stretcher. It probably suffered its water damage during the war whilst in storage at White and Co. Ltd Furniture Depositories, Portsmouth. The picture joined the museum collection in 1998.

The Governor's Green, Portsmouth,
1860.

THIS quaint old painting by Ubsdell depicts Portsmouth at the height of its glory, when the fashionable world was centred in the old town. The scene here shows us the Officers of the Garrison with their ladies, promenading on the Green, and the Townsfolk gathered on the Ramparts, all listening to the Regimental Band. On the right, a portion of the Chancel of the Garrison Church and the old Mortar can be seen. Behind this, the long Curtain, and to the left of the Band the entrance that led to the Spur Redoubt. The flag is flying on the King's Bastion, and the adjoining ramparts (behind the elm trees) formed part of King's Ravelin. King William Gate, with Guard House, is across Green Row (now Pembroke Road) and was pulled down in 1870. Pembroke Chapel can be recognized, but the Naval Club was not then built. Following along we get the gun shop—still in existence, and then the residence of the artist, who has portrayed himself looking out of a window. Unfortunately modern improvements have swept away this picturesque scene.

R.H.C. Ubsdell, Governor's Green
(PMRS 1998/276)

A - Ubsdell's House, 1 Green Row

B - Gun Shop

C - (1st) Royal Naval Club

D - Inn

E - Green Row Assembly Rooms & School

F - Wine Merchants

G - Pembroke Chapel

H - 'Trafalgar House'

I - King William IV Gate

R.H.C. Ubsdell, 'Trafalgar House' King William IV Gate
(PMRS 1998/276)

A CELEBRATION OF UBSDELL'S SUCCESS

Ubsdell painted the picture in 1860. The success of his photography business had enabled him to move to surely the grandest house in Portsmouth. The scene is viewed from an elevated position, most likely the upstairs room of the Little Blue Posts public house where he was born.

From the place of Ubsdell's birth in poverty the painting shows him admiring the view from the upstairs of his new house, along with his wife and one of his sons in the other windows.

The painting looks towards the King William IV Gate. The road then crossed the moat towards Southsea and Hambrook Street, where his brother William Chinn was building his hairdressing, perfume and stationery businesses.

R.H.C. Ubsdell, The King's Bastion Governor's Green
(PMRS 1998/276)

NELSON'S LAST JOURNEY

Governor's Green portrays the route of Nelson's last journey on 14th September 1805. On this day he left The George Hotel in Portsmouth High Street by the back entrance, walked down Penny Street turned the corner into Green Row, walked past what would become Ubsdell's house to the 'Trafalgar House' where his sister lived. Having bid her goodbye he would have crossed Governor's Green by the path in the picture and would have passed through the tunnel to the right of the King's bastion and crossed by a bridge over the moat to the Spur Redoubt, and thence to the beach and a boat that was to take him to The Victory anchored off Stokes Bay Gosport.

Ubsdell recorded the aftermath of the Crimea War, and a number of wood engravings based on his sketches of the troops returning home appeared in the Illustrated London papers. The 1860s also saw a renewed fear of invasion from France, and new Forts were built up on the Portsdown Ridge to the North of the town and out in the approaches to the harbour:- the so called 'Palmerston Follies'. Renewed patriotism led to the formation of Volunteer Regiments, and their parades were to be a considerable spectacle. Ubsdell recorded the reviews at Hyde Park and at Winchester in 1860 (now believed lost) and a review below the Portsdown Ridge that included mock attacks on the forts above in 1868. In 1863 Ubsdell recorded four scenes of celebration in Portsmouth at the marriage of Edward, the Prince of Wales and Princess Alexandra of Denmark, and presented them to the Prince & Princess when they returned from honeymoon at Osborne on the Isle of Wight. Ubsdell had been given the job of creating the ceremonial scroll of address, and recording the moment of its presentation to the Prince & Princess by the Corporation of Portsmouth.

Ubsdell's final topographical views were created for, and with, the widow Lady Fetherstonhaugh and her sister Frances between 1864 and 1878, and show views on the Uppark estate.

Modern Bridge connecting Nelson's tunnel with the Spur Redoubt

With Ubsdell's growing success, and to expand his photography business, in 1859 Ubsdell moved to possibly the best house in Portsmouth, 1 Green Row. Ubsdell occupied the double-fronted cream coloured building, and part of the building on the corner with its red mansard roof. It is currently the residence of the Dean of Portsmouth.

Ubsdell's picture opposite exhibited at the Royal Academy in 1849 shows 2186 men of the Royal Dockyard Volunteer Battalion drinking a toast to the queen proposed by Rear-Admiral Prescott CB. The occasion is the opening by Queen Victoria of the New Steam Basin for the construction and repair of steam powered naval ships; a programme that had begun in 1843, 5 years earlier.

Ships were becoming longer. Steam was taking over from Sail as an auxiliary, or main means of propulsion, steel hulls were taking over from wood, shell firing turrets were taking over from cannon, screw propulsion from paddle wheels. A great many different configurations were being built and evaluated.

No 2 dry dock which today houses HMS Victory, and No 3 dry dock, which houses the remains of The Mary Rose are accessed from the Great Ship Basin (No 1 Basin) dating back to 1704. The Steam Basin (No 2 Basin) was originally accessed by means of an entrance to its North, and later from a caisson type gate to the East. Dry docks 8 and 11 were accessed from the basin, and dry dock 7 which when used in conjunction with dry dock 10 provided another means of access, and the latter two when used together, the only means of placing a ship of the length of HMS Warrior in dry dock. In the Dreadnought era three later basins were combined to create Basin No 3.

As part of the 1843 scheme Boathouse No 6 was constructed for the storage and maintenance of ships' boats. Boats could access the boathouse from the pond in front, which had been originally used for the storage of ships masts, and which links to the harbour by means of a tunnel. The feast took place on the first floor of the building. Today the Boathouse is open to the public and forms the 'Action Stations' exhibit, it has been extensively rebuilt at the rear following bomb damage in World War II. In the rebuilding the opportunity was taken to include a 275 seat auditorium in the roof together with a futuristic fire escape.

Boathouse No6

R.H.C. Ubsdell, In Boathouse No 6 Rear Admiral Prescott proposing to the Royal Dockyard Battalion a toast to Queen Victoria on the occasion of the opening of the Steam Basin 25th May 1848
(PMRS 1973/1185)

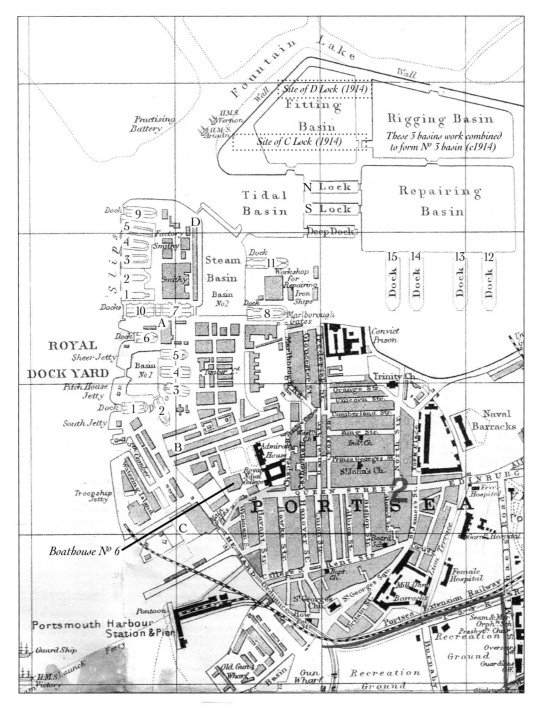

On the day of the opening Queen Victoria and Prince Albert arrived on the Royal Yacht Fairy at 3.10. The yacht performed a circuit of the basin before the Queen disembarked to participate in a stone-laying ceremony, after which the Fairy performed another circuit of the basin before returning the Couple to Osborne.

With standing room for 20,000, the dockyard workers and navvies lined the basin. For those with tickets there were also 21 booths with seats, and viewing positions at the windows of the new Steam Factory that ran down the Western edge of the basin. 1050 navvies of contractor Peter Rolt sat down for their meal in this Factory. Unlimited beer was available so this party did not break up until midnight.

The party in Ubsdell's picture was more subdued and finished at 9pm. Two orchestras took it in turns to play at either end off the hall.

There were 17 tables each 160 feet long. The cold fare in 1455 dishes consisted of roast and boiled beef, veal and hams, legs and shoulders of mutton, quarters of lamb, meat pies, salads, plum puddings, bread, mustard and ale.

KEY
A - Marc Isambard Brunel's Block Mills
(M.I. Brunel was the father of Isambard Kingdom Brunel)
B - The Great Ropery
C - HMS Warrior 1860
D - Steam Factory

Docks
1 - HMS Monitor 1915
2 - HMS Victory 1765
3 - Mary Rose

Map c. 1910 annotated to show Slips, Locks, Docks, Basins and major feeatures.

Boathouse No. 6 was mainly designed by Major General Roger Stewart Beatson (1812 -1896) of the Royal Engineers, when still a Lieutenant, with an outside engineer being used for the roof design. The Boathouse was designed on three floors for the maintenance and construction of ancillary ships boats. A flow-line system operated whereby boats could be taken to the top floor by means of pulleys, and then progressively make their way through the required work stations, back down to the ground floor. Beatson designed the boathouse with wide spans, so as to have as much unimpeded floor-space as possible.

Beatson supported his floors with massive cast-iron beams. Cast-iron was a comparatively cheap material. It is very strong under compressive loads, so the supporting cast iron columns could be fairly slender. However, cast-iron is weak under tension. When loaded, a beam will tend to bend, causing the bottom of the beam to stretch and become tensioned. To prevent this happening Bateson used wrought-iron tensioning bars, attached with iron pins to either side of the mid-point of the beam, to tie-back the centre of the beam to its own ends. In this way Bateson calculated that each beam could take a load of 40 tons. The wrought-iron bars were installed hot, so that as they cooled they would shrink, creating enough tension to stop the beams bending under their own weight and that of the empty building. The cast iron beams themselves merely slotted together on top of their cast iron columns.

Cast iron beams slot together

Engineers were very aware of the limitations of cast-iron after Robert Stephenson's Dee Bridge had collapsed in 1847, due to torsional loads on the beams created by ill-considered bracing. After Boathouse No. 6 was constructed there was to be another famous cast-iron bridge failure. In 1879 the Tay Bridge collapsed. This is thought to have been due to metal fatigue in insufficient lugs that joined the wrought-iron tension bars to the flanges on the cast-iron support columns, by means of round metal bolts of insufficient diameter. It is hard to imagine the tensioning system in Boathouse No. 6 suffering a similar fate.

Cast iron beam with wrought iron tension bars

"Action Stations' inside Boat House No. 6

THE WEDDING OF EDWARD AND ALEXANDRA
10TH MARCH 1863

The date is Tuesday 10th March 1863. The time is 8pm. The location is Green Row Portsmouth looking towards St Thomas's Church (now Portsmouth Cathedral) and Portsmouth High Street. The occasion is a celebration of the marriage of His Royal Highness Albert Edward Prince of Wales and Her Royal Highness The Princess Alexandra Caroline of Denmark.

The Royal Yacht Victoria & Albert, together with the Royal Yacht Osborne, the steamer Vivid, and the Trinity Yacht had conveyed the princess's party from Antwerp on Thursday the 5th. Warships Revenge & Warrior joined the fleet outside The Scheldt and the fleet anchored in Margate Roads around 11 o'clock that night, and at half past two the next day the Princess received an address from Margate Corporation. The fleet anchored again at The Nore on the night of the 6th before arriving at Gravesend on the morning of Saturday the 7th. She was met by the Prince at Gravesend and went from thence by train to Bricklayers' Arms Station. Then followed a procession through London via London Bridge, The Mansion House, St Paul's, Temple Bar, Trafalgar Square, Pall Mall, Hyde Park, by train from Paddington to Slough, and thence by carriage through Eton to Windsor. On every part of their journey the Prince and Princess were met by huge crowds seizing the chance for a national celebration after the misery of the Crimean War and the death of the Prince Consort less than two years before. The wedding took place in St George's Chapel on the morning of March 10th. The Royal Couple finally departed from Windsor station of the Great Western Railway and via Reading arrived at Southampton at 6pm where the ships of the Peninsular and Oriental Company were dressed out in flags. The Royal Couple descended to The Royal Barge which conveyed the couple to The Royal Yacht which in turn took them to The Trinity House Landing Pier at Cowes. Then followed a week's honeymoon at Osborne.

Prince Edward
Chromo-lithographs by Robert Dudley

The Wedding at Windsor
Chromo-lithographs by Robert Dudley

Princess Alexandra
Chromo-lithographs by Robert Dudley

The Royal Couple returned via Portsmouth on board the smallest Royal Yacht – The Fairy. At Portsmouth they were received on board the yacht by the Mayor, Mr W. G. Chambers, The Town Clerk, Mr Hellard, the Rev. J.P. Stigant, the Mace Bearer Mr Martell, the Town Crier, and R.H.C. Ubsdell and who had prepared the congratulatory address, and who recorded the scene in a painting. The painting was subsequently exhibited at Ubsdell's house from where you could buy a photograph of it if you wished. Ultimately this painting probably found its way to the Town Hall, latterly the museum, on the High Street that was destroyed by German bombing in WW2. Ubsdell, always one to seize an opportunity, presented 4 watercolour paintings of the wedding day celebrations in Portsmouth to the Prince and Princess, and these have survived in The Royal Collection to this day.

The Newcastle Courant reported on 10th July 1863 that:

'On the occasion of her Majesty crossing from Portsmouth harbour to Osborne in the royal screw yacht Fairy, Captain his Serene Highness Prince Leiningen submitted to her Majesty's inspection a cabinet watercolour drawing, by Mr Ubsdell, artist, of Portsmouth representing the presentation of the Portsmouth corporate address on the deck of the Fairy to the Prince and Princess of Wales, on the arrival of their Royal Highnesses in the yacht off the entrance to Portsmouth, en route from Osborne to Windsor. Her Majesty is understood to have expressed herself much pleased with the truthfulness of the Prince and Princess, and also with the artistic manner in which the subject had been rendered.'

Ubsdell had presumably used his contacts in the Royal Yacht Squadron to get his paintings in the hands of Prince Leiningen who was an honorary member there, and captain of the biggest royal yacht the Victoria & Albert. Unfortunately for Ubsdell he probably chose the wrong media for his picture. At this time Queen Victoria was an ardent collector of 'miniatures' (some actually quite enormous) on ivory, and if Ubsdell had painted on ivory rather than paper, Queen Victoria would probably have bought the picture!

The first of the four records the celebrations at 3pm on Southsea Common where nearly 12,000 Portsmouth school children assembled to hear an address by The Mayor before they advanced to sing "God Save The Queen", and then disbursed for refreshments at their various Portsmouth schools. The next picture records the evening's events, the Royal Yacht proceeding to the IOW with the fleet illuminated by blue lamps along their yardarms and each ship firing

R.H.C. Ubsdell, Free School Children advancing to sing "God Save the Queen" at Portsmouth. 10th March 1863.
Supplied by Royal Collection Trust / © HM Queen Elizabeth II 2012

R.H.C. Ubsdell, The Royal couple receiving Ubsdell's Illuminated Address from Portsmouth Corporation.

"20 long lights, 26 shells, 32 firework mortars, 20 golden rain shells, 20 tail shells, 20 crackers, 20 squib shells, 20 assorted shells and 100 rockets". The third painting records the bonfire and fireworks on Southsea Common, with the tar barrels on poles set on fire along the promenade. It manages to capture the rain and blustery conditions that briefly managed to dampen the activities.

For us however it is the scene of Green Row that is the most interesting. What Ubsdell chooses to include in the picture tells us so much about him. On the right is part of his house, 1 Green Row. At this date the corner site is clearly part of the main property, and I suspect where the flag is on the right edge of the picture there would have been a small passage-way through to a yard and a stable at the back. Then there came the main double-fronted house, 3 windows either side of the front door. I think subsequently the house would have lost some land at the back, the passage-way filled in with a house side extension, and a revised fascia built with small triangular canopies over the windows and a stone balustrade in front of the roof pitch. When the freehold was sold on 8th May 1875 the building on the corner was still part of the property and formed part of the frontage, but possibly part of the corner block was then being let to Mr Cook as business premises along with 33 and 34 Penny

R.H.C. Ubsdell, The Illuminetion of St. Thomas's Church Portsmouth. 10th March 1963.
Supplied by Royal Collection Trust / © HM Queen Elizabeth II 2012

Street. The corner property has been rebuilt subsequently acquiring a mansard roof, but still retains a revised 1st floor bay window.

The bay window is Ubsdell's abat-jour (light collector/deflector) so this would have been his photographic studio. The decorations that span the street over to Governor's Green and those which decorate his studio were of Ubsdell's own design and construction, while those that span Pembroke Street in the background emanate from no 2 Pembroke Street which was the property of fellow artist, photographer, teacher, and art supplies retailer, Richard Poate. On the left is the Little Blue Posts public house, and the illuminated first floor window is the room in which we suspect RHC was born. This building still exists but it subsequently acquired a second storey. The illuminated windows at street level could have been the dining rooms where Richard senior was a waiter and kitchen porter. The building with the triangular pediment was the Green Row facade of the Town Hall built to replace the historic Town Hall and market that had inconveniently occupied the middle of the High Street. At street level in this building there was a police station and a Market Hall where shortly before his death Richard senior sold perfume. On the other corner of Green Row and Penny Street was a shop unit which in part of its life was occupied by Charpentier, the stationers, map, and picture sellers. The flares on St Thomas's were supplied by the Mayor.

UBSDELL AS A PHOTOGRAPHER

Ubsdell's studio at 1, Green Row enabled him to make a good living from the craze for photographic visiting cards, carte-de-visite, that was raging at the time. He also did stereoscopic and other views of local sites. One of his photographs which has survived is that of the western church yard of St. Thomas's around 1860. We can identify the picture from the church building that still exists in St. Thomas's Street behind.

Church owned houses in St Thomas's St

St. Thomas's western churchyard c1860, destroyed in the war
(David Quinton)

Ubsdell's Portraits

Ubsdell was primarily a portrait artist but whereas his watercolour paintings of churches stayed together as collections, his portraits are dispersed in family collections. His practice of signing portraits by means of brown paper labels stuck to the frame or presentation box has meant that many portraits that are surely by him cannot be positively identified. Here though are 3 portraits that can be positively identified in three different media spanning 35 years of Ubsdell's output.

Dr John Sinclair (1) was Assistant Surgeon at HMS Excellent the Royal Navy gunnery school at Portsmouth which at this time consisted of a series of hulks in the Fareham Creek at Portsmouth. He had been posted to HMS Rattlesnake in 1839 but for some reason did not take up the posting. This was unfortunate for him as on 25th October 1840 he suffered an accident having been thrown from a horse drawn gig on a journey from Southampton to Titchfield. He had won a raffle the previous day and had won a statue of 'Old Mortality and his Pony' based on the Sir Walter Scott novel. His parents erected the statue as a memorial to him which can still be seen today as part of Dumfries Museum in Scotland. This was an early example of Naval officers shown as portraits on board ship and would lead to similar work being used for Ackermann's 'Royal Navy' series of Aquatints in 1849.

Sir Walter de Winton (2) is seen newly returned from the Crimea where he served in the trenches as part of the siege and fall of Savastopol. He received the medal with clasp and the Turkish medal and was made a Knight of the Legion of Honour. Less gloriously he was in 1880 administrator of King Leopold's private kingdom of the Congo. He administered various British Imperial territories before finally becoming controller and treasurer of the households of firstly the Duke of Clarence, and then the Duke of York.

(1) Dr John Sinclair MD, Assistant Surgeon, HMS Excellent, Portsmouth June 30th 1840 (66 x 51 cm) Watercolour on Paper. Signed Lower Left and with a brown paper label on the mount.

Sir Houston Stewart (3) had an illustrious naval career which included serving with Lord Cochrane (the inspiration for the Hornblower novels) in the Impérieuse. In the Crimea he was second in command in the Black Sea under Sir Edmund Lyons and was responsible for the capture of Kinburn. Ubsdell would first have met him in 1839 when he recorded a feast to celebrate the return of Admiral Sir Robert Stopford from the Mediterranean. Stewart had commanded off the coast of Syria and was present at the capture of Acre. He became rear-admiral in 1851, vice-admiral in 1857, admiral in 1862 and admiral of the fleet in 1872. The oil portrait was probably painted after death, the image taken from a glass negative, from which Ubsdell Studio had produced cartes-de-visite some years earlier.

(2) Major General Sir Francis Walter de Winton as a Lieutenant 1856 (20 x 15 cm) Watercolour 'Miniature' on ivory Signed below the mount. (Private Collection)

(3) The Late Admiral of the Fleet Sir Houston Stewart (1791-1875) MP (circa 1875) (97 x 80 cm) Oil Painting. Identified and signed by a brown paper label on the frame in Ubsdell's hand.

Another naval captain that had served with Lord Cochrane was Frederick Marryat (1792-1848) the novelist, contemporary and acquaintance of Charles Dickens. His most famous novel was 'Mr Midshipman Easy' (1836):- still a remarkably refreshing and interesting 'read' today.

His eldest son Frederick (4) was, when he was young, like his father, a spirited young man who would cause his father anguish, but would nevertheless want to make him proud. One day in June 1842, probably as a newly appointed lieutenant, he would have entered Ubsdell's studio for a celebratory portrait. Ubsdell would have sketched the features of the head, making the surrounding area black with his pencil. Later he would have quickly filled in the rest of the detail in watercolour as a preparatory study for an oil painting. The shaded area around the head would have been turned into the curtain.

What then happened to this watercolour study before coming into the possession of the National Maritime Museum we don't know but Lieutenant Frederick Marryat's fate we do know. He was drowned at sea in 1848. He was lost when the paddle wheel frigate HMS Avenger (1845) captained by Charles Elers Napier, stepson of Rear Admiral Charles Napier, ran onto the Sorelle Rocks near Malta. Lieutenant Marryat was swept overboard whilst trying to clear away the ship's boats.

News of his son's death reached his novelist father during a serious illness and he too died shortly afterwards.

(4) Frederick Marryat son of the author Captain Marryat (National Maritime Museum PAF 6285) (Note: signature may be that of younger brother Dan Ubsdell 1817-46)

Ubsdell accumulated preparatory drawings and sketches of many famous people and events. When he took to photography he built a library of glass slides of local sites and personalities. These could be useful to other artists and lithograpers.

The disconnected way in which the faces in the official oil portraits of the Earl of Yarborough and Charles Sumner, Bishop of Winchester scarcely belong to their bodies, suggests that in fact these portraits were based on miniatures by the artist who knew them best, R.H.C. Ubsdell.

(5) Lord Frederick FitzClarence, lithograph after R.H.C. Ubsdell, 1850s (NPG D36939)

Lord Frederick FitzClarence (5) (9th Dec 1799 – 30th Oct 1854) was the third illegitimate son of King William IV and his mistress, Dorothea Jordan. Between 1847 and 1851 he was Lieutenant-Governor of Portsmouth. Clarence Esplanade opened in 1848 is named after him. Before giving up his command of Lieutenant Governor he presented the town on 18th June 1850 with statues, now lost, of Lord Nelson & the Duke of Wellington. Ubsdell recorded the event in a painting, now also lost. Here was another opportunity for Ubsdell to add to his library of images of famous people. It has survived as a lithograph in the National Portrait Gallery Collection, lithography by James Henry Lynch and printed by Day & Son.

From preparatory drawings such as that of Dr John Sinclair (p xx) Ubsdell could compile composite watercolours of scenes of officers and ratings posed on board Royal Navy ships.

In 1849 the London printmakers Ackermann & Co. (1795-c1990) issued an edition of aquatints entitled 'The Royal Navy' (6) based on original watercolours by R.H.C. Ubsdell. (Aquatints simulated a range of greys by fusing grains of rosin to selected parts of a metal plate, and exposing the resulting plate to acid for different lengths of times. Those parts of the plate not protected by the grains of rosin, when bitten by acid, would produce a grey tone, when inked up and printed. Those parts of the plate exposed for longer times had a darker tone). The skilled engraver was John Harris (1811-1865). There were 6 in the series and subscribers bought 2 a month in May, June, and July 1849. No. 4 in the series is unique in the National Maritime Museum collection for having Ubsdell's original watercolour, a example just in grey tones, and a beautiful hand-coloured version. A complete hand-coloured set was sold at Christies on 7 Jun 2000 and made £5,640, the highest price yet paid for an Ubsdell.

No. 2 in the series featured left-to-right Commander, Captain, Midshipman and Admiral. It is most interesting as the Admiral is surely none other than Jane Austen's eldest brother Sir Francis Austen (7). A painting exists in a private collection of Sir Francis in the full-dress uniform of a Vice-Admiral painted soon after his promotion at the time of Queen Victoria's Coronation in June 1838. This first appeared in print in the book 'Jane Austen's Sailor Brothers' by J.H.Hubback & E.C. Hubback in 1906. Sir Francis would have been well known in Portsmouth as he lived at Portsdown Lodge, just outside the town, on the original London Road, and was a director of the Portsmouth Floating Bridge Company.

(7) Vice-Admiral Sir Francis Austen K.C.B. (From a painting in the possession of Mrs Herbert Austen) from Jane Austen's Sailor Brothers J.H. & E.C. Hubback 1906

(6) The Royal Navy No. 2, Aquatint, 'Commander, Captain, Midshipman, Admiral', May 1849 after R.H.C. Ubsdell (National Maritime Museum PW4223)

GRAND NAVAL FUNERAL OF CAPTAIN SIR HENRY MARTIN BLACKWOOD, 2ND BARONET BLACKWOOD, OF H.M.S. "VENGEANCE" PORTSMOUTH HARBOUR

There are memorials at Portsmouth to Captain Sir Henry Martin Blackwood in both St. Ann's Church that lies within the Historic Dockyard, and the Royal Garrison Church.

On Saturday 11th January, Portsmouth turned out for a remarkable public funeral procession to mark the death of the forty nine year old newly appointed Captain of the Vengeance, a very fast 84 gun second-rate ship of the Canopus Class.

Blackwood had had an exemplary career, but his funeral was about much more than the Navy and Army paying respects to a young captain cut down in his prime, probably with cancer, for Henry Martin Blackwood was the only son of Vice-Admiral Sir Henry Blackwood, 1st Baronet, GCH, KCB (28th Dec 1770 – 17th Dec 1832). His father had been present at Trafalgar.

Vice-Admiral Blackwood had been Nelson's 'eyes and ears' before Trafalgar. He commanded the frigate Euryalus of 36 guns and had brought the news to London that Vice-Admiral Villeneuve had taken his fleet to Cadiz. Nelson returned to sea and put Blackwood in command of the inshore squadron of frigates watching for Villeneuve to leave harbour, and pass on signals to the Victory. Nelson sought a decisive victory against the Combined French & Spanish Fleet that would remove the risk of invasion once and for all. Before the battle Blackwood and Captain Hardy of the Victory had witnessed Nelson's codicil to his Will, commending the care of his mistress Emma Lady Hamilton and his daughter by her, Horatia, to the protection of a grateful Nation. The Nation was to cruelly ignore this last request.

On 18th October 1805 Villeneuve's fleet begins its departure from Cadiz bound for Naples. Nelson brings his fleet in position to engage the enemy. Around 12.10 p.m. on 21st Oct 1805 with the enemy fleets beginning to exchange shots, Blackwood left the Victory to return to his own ship. He took Nelson's hand saying, 'I trust, my Lord, that on my return to the Victory, which shall be as soon as possible, I shall find your Lordship well, and in possession of twenty prizes'. Nelson responded, 'God bless you Blackwood, I shall never speak to you again'.

Troops from the garrison lined Portsmouth High Street all the way down from the George Hotel to the Royal Victoria Pier, and the coffin was carried on the shoulders of men from the Vengeance, followed in procession by all remaining military and naval personnel in the town.

The Illustrated London News of 18th Jan 1851 carried the story:-

'On the arrival at the Victoria Pier, the barges and boats of the ships were in attendance to receive the Body and the cortège. The band of the 82nd Royal Marine Artillery and the guard of honour occupied the first boat; in the second were the Body, and the pallbearers and mourners; in the (next six boats) officers of Navy and Army. On either side of the principal barges were escorts of boats, all having the white ensign at half-mast. The procession crossed the harbour's mouth, the bands playing the "Dead March", and the Vengeance commenced firing "minute guns". The appearance of the ship in mourning had a solemn effect; the yards were lowered, and all signs of white were obliterated'.

The party then proceeded to the Haslar Jetty to be met by the corps of The Royal Marines for a service at Haslar Hospital chapel and burial in the Haslar graveyard.

(Right) Meeting/Funeral of Henry Blackwood of the Vengeance 11 Jan 1851
(ILN 18 Jan 1851 p37 NMM PR62:256)

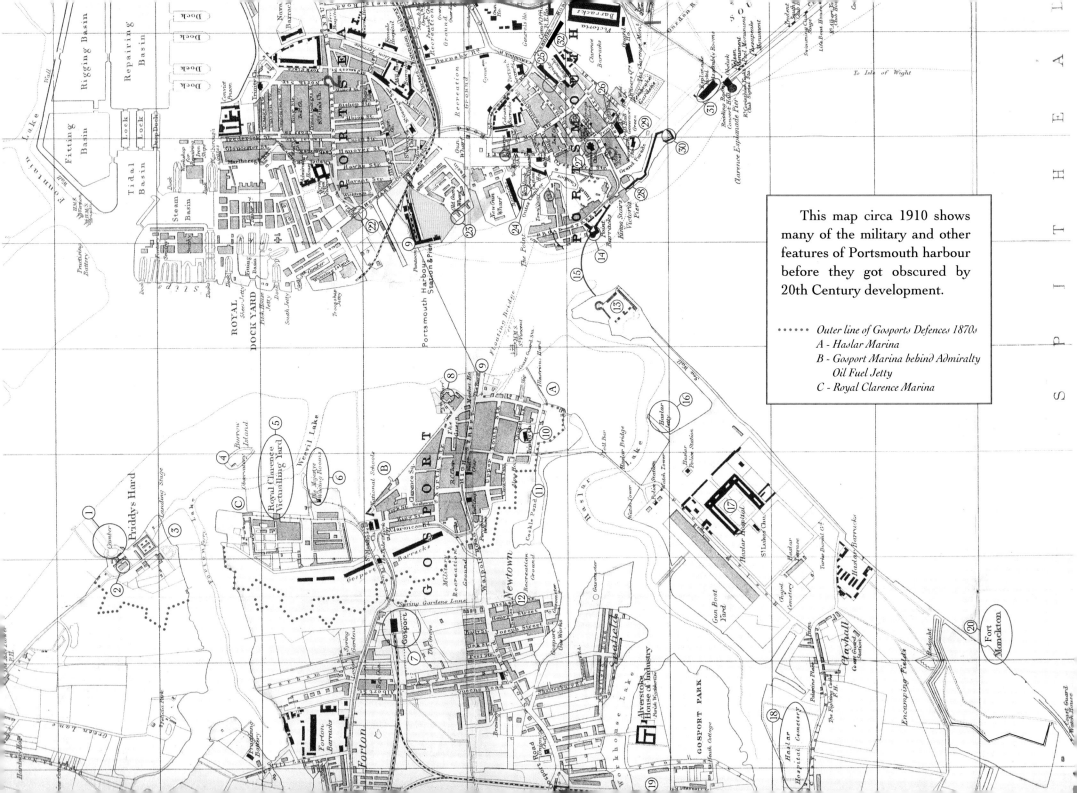

This map circa 1910 shows many of the military and other features of Portsmouth harbour before they got obscured by 20th Century development.

...... *Outer line of Gosports Defences 1870s*
A - Haslar Marina
B - Gosport Marina behind Admiralty Oil Fuel Jetty
C - Royal Clarence Marina

Gosport Peninsula

KEY
• • • • • • •
Eclipse
Bus Rapid Transit Road

Gosport is a fascinating place although it is easy to be put off by the dreary east side of the peninsula and the slow crawl to get through the traffic around Fareham and the slow crawl down the A32. It is to be hoped that the Eclipse Rapid Transit Road for buses and cyclists on the old railway line between Tichborne Way in Gosport and Redlands Lane in Fareham will do something to reduce congestion. The southern section of the railway line is a cycle and footpath, as is the branch line that used to go down to a pier at Stokes Bay for steamers to Ryde on the Isle of Wight. Gosport station has been converted into apartments and offices.

The west side of the peninsula is a delightful sanctuary with its views over the Solent to the Isle of Wight, and the coast road as far as Titchfield Haven.

(1) The Camber Harbour Priddy's Hard

The Anglesey Hotel is a wonderful place to stay and venture out to explore little known fascinating places, which may have somewhat restricted opening hours. You may wish to time a visit to coincide with the annual open day of the Hovercraft Museum, or Heritage Weekend in September when all the attractions will most probably be open. The tourist office near the Portsmouth Ferry terminal on Gosport Hard is a good place to browse a wide range of local history publications, and find out more, especially about the military offensive and defensive heritage of the area.

Anglesey was named after Henry Paget, 2nd Earl of Uxbridge, who was styled Lord Paget between 1784 and 1812 and following his heroic actions at Waterloo was created the Marquess of Anglesey by the Prince Regent in July 1815. Paget had commanded the whole of the allied cavalry and horse artillery at Waterloo and after having eight or nine horses shot from under him was himself hit in the leg by a cannon shot in the closing stages and had to have his right leg amputated above the knee.

Gosport Peninsula

(16) HMS Alliance Submarine Museum Gosport

Ubsdell's patron Sir Frederic Madden had been born in Portsmouth on 16th February 1801 at his father's house at 31 St. Thomas's Street. He left Portsmouth in 1824 to begin his career at The British Museum, but he maintained links with the town, and Gosport, where his sister Clarissa Harriet lived near the Stoke Road station. Madden would have been particularly interested in Ubsdell preserving a record of Charles Fort that would at one time have dominated the Hard at Gosport, and reconstructing an image of Gosport Chapel before the Binghams became incumbents and Thomas Ellis Owen had undertaken his heavy handed repairs and rebuilding of its west end.

Between 1836 and 1840 Ubsdell had been employed by John Deane ,co-inventor with his brother of the diving helmet, in illustrating his recoveries from The Mary Rose and other sunken shipwrecks. The pioneering work of Deane and the history of diving equipment is told in the recently opened Diving Museum at Battery No. 2 in Stokes Bay.

The Diving Museum at No. 2 Battery Stokes Bay Lines.

R.H.C. Ubsdell, Charles Fort, 1841
(PMRS 1945/419/27)

Charles Fort (map no. 8) and James Fort (map no. 4) were completed by 1679 and were part of Sir Bernard de Gomme's plans for the fortifications of Portsmouth harbour. The forts were designed to protect the dockyard (map no. 21) and could direct fire on enemy forces that had managed to get past Fort Blockhouse and the chain boom (map no. 13 and 14).

Charles Fort, known as the 'Great Redoubt' stood on the quay at Gosport in the region of the current Falklands Gardens and the start of Gosport Marina. Ubsdell's watercolours are of the central tower, which had two floors of standing height. Overall it would appear to be about 5m high and about 8m square and would have provided the ammunition store and sleeping accommodation for the men who manned it. There were cannons on the roof, and the remains of ornamental towers can be seen at the corners of the roofline. Surrounding the central tower would have been earthwork parapets in a square forming the lower battery, where the majority of the cannon were placed, in all possibly as many as 30. The stone facings on the parapet were probably quickly plundered for building material when the fort fell into disuse. The openings in one of the walls look like passageways and stairways, suggesting that the fort may have been incorporated into another building when it had outlived its original purpose.

R.H.C. Ubsdell, Charles Fort, 1841
(PMRS 1945/419/25)

R.H.C. Ubsdell, Charles Fort, 1841
(PMRS 1945/419/26)

Site of Charles Fort, Gosport side of Haslar Marina

Site of Charles Fort, Falklands Gardens Gosport

Gosport Chapel HOLY TRINTY

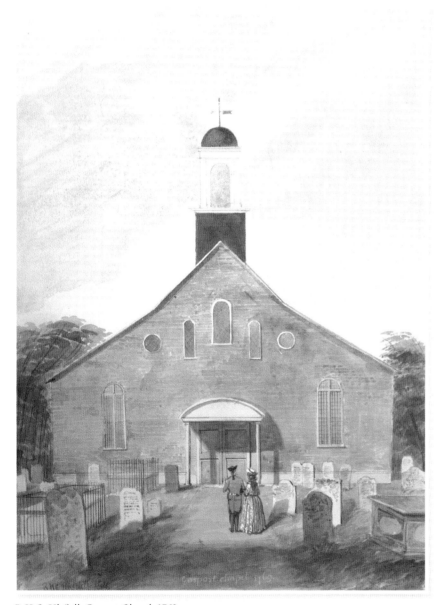

R.H.C. Ubsdell, Gosport Chapel, 1769
(PMRS 1945/419/24)

Ubsdell's watercolour sold to Madden in 1842, and which the church most proudly displays on their website shows a historic view said to be of the church in 1769. The significance of the date is unclear. Perhaps the date should be 1779 when the well-connected Rev. Isaac Moody Bingham was licensed to Holy Trinity, or 1789 when his son the Rev. Richard Bingham began serving his father as curate, before being licensed in 1792 as the church's new incumbent, whereupon he continued to hold the position for an incredible 66 years, (although his son Richard acted as his curate from 1822-44) until succeeded by Rev. Skipsey Saunders in 1858. Most probably the date represents a period a decade before any of the Binghams came to the parish.

The church guide refers to Richard Bingham's tenure as years of 'fame and infamy'. In 1795 he obtained a grant of land from the east of the church to the waterfront from the Lord of the Manor, the notoriously corrupt Brownlow North, Bishop of Winchester. On this land he built a magnificent vicarage. The church guide says Bingham was only to enjoy his vicarage for a couple of years 'before the Board of Ordnance acquired it as the residence of the commandant of Royal Engineers. This did not happen without a struggle as Bingham embarked on one of his many Court appearances. He later came to an agreement with the army, selling his interests in the land for £15,000 and leasing the house for £100 per year. He straightaway (then) started building (another) new vicarage to the east of the church. This was to remain a vicarage until 1858, after

Holy Trinity

which it became the home of Mr Benjamin Nicholson, head of the famous yacht builders. It was demolished in 1962.

⊗⊛⊗

Piecing together more of the story it would appear that Bingham misused his position as trustee of a charity to mortgage its property to finance his various speculations and schemes. He also had the income from other ecclesiastical posts including Canon of the Cathedral Church of Chichester and the parish of Hale Magna, Sleaford, Lincolnshire; although he had to give up the living of Maresfield, Sussex after being accused of writing threatening letters to his parishoners, and setting fire to his own house in order to claim on the insurance. He owned a disreputable public house on Beach Street backing onto the harbour and allegedly a front for smuggling activities. In 1813 he served six months in prison in Winchester for evading stamp duty on a house conveyance. This is all despite being a Hampshire Magistrate of 12 years standing! Bingham bought land just outside Gosport's fortifications between the Stoke Road and Haslar Lake in 1807 and on it built a variety of houses in streets named after some of his sons, Richard, Henry, Joseph and Charles. The area is still referred to as 'Bingham Town' or 'Newtown'. After re-development the names of Henry and Joseph Streets still exist on paper but are now mere alleys.

⊗⊛⊗

The church guide carries a photograph of a very heavy late Georgian west end to the church, most probably the Thomas Ellis Owen enlargement and repairs of 1829. So it would appear that Madden commissioned the picture to show how things were before the changes wrought by Southsea's famous architect and Gosport's most notorious clergyman.

⊗⊛⊗

The rebuilding of Sir Arthur Blomfield that started in 1886 can probably be seen as undoing Bingham's and Owen's changes and reverting to something much closer to Ubsdell's watercolour. The exterior became an Italian Lombard Style and Blomfield faced the original stucco with red Mathematical tiles and revised the bell cote. The remarkable tall isolated campanile bell and clock tower was added by Blomfield in 1889, and by then the west end had assumed its modern aspect.

⊗⊛⊗

The interior of Holy Trinity is most beautiful. The church was founded as a result of the growth of Gosport and the need to avoid the often hazardous journey to the church at Alverstoke. The Lord of the Manor at the time was Peter Mews, Bishop of Winchester who granted the land, and from his estate of Farnham Castle donated 14 oak trees which, now encased, support the roof to this day. The pride of the church is the organ commissioned by Handel when employed by James Brydges, Duke of Chandos in 1717-18. The organ was installed at Cannons on his estate near Edgware, Middlesex. Chandos had amassed great wealth as paymaster-general to British troops abroad in the war of the Spanish Succession, but lost money invested in the South Sea and York Buildings Companies thereby getting deeply in debt. The result was that the 2nd Duke of Chandos demolished Cannons and sold the remains of the building and its contents. Holy Trinity purchased the organ for £117 when Camons was demolished in 1744. With the death of the 3rd Duke of Chandos in 1789 the title became extinct, and it was this title that Samuel Egerton Brydges brother of Anne Brydges (Madam Lefroy the friend of Jane Austen) tried unsuccessfully to claim. On the north side of the church is a memorial to six of the fifteen children of Henry Needham Scrope Shrapnel (1812-1896) four of whom died within 3 months of each other between December 1843 and March 1844. Shrapnel was the son of Lieutenant General Henry Shrapnel (1761-1842), of the Royal Artillery inventor of the long range explosive fragmentation shell that bears his name. Scrope Shrapnel was a barrack-master in Ireland, Bermuda, Halifax and Montreal, who settled in Orilla, Ontario, Canada on his retirement in 1866, and where he died almost penniless.

⊗⊛⊗

The church is most proud of its 'high church' Anglo-Catholicism tradition commenced by the Rev. William Skipsey-Saunders when he embraced the ethos of the Oxford Movement with its emphasis on ritual and ceremony.

Alverstoke ST. MARY'S

Ubsdell's watercolour adds greatly to our knowledge of the history of this church. Sue Pike in her book on Thomas Ellis Owen narrates his involvement in church architecture. She notes that the architect 'refurbished' the church between 1830 and 1832. Ubsdell's watercolour shows clearly where the church was repaired in red brick. The tower acquired battlements and a little circular tower. The chapel to the side has been increased in height and re-roofed. Beyond the chapel we see the chancel. On the other side of the line of trees is a path with a brick wall separating the church from Church Road.

Owen would have overseen the work whilst he was supervising construction of his first major architectural commission, his elegant Nash styled crescent in Crescent Road that faced the sea, one road back from Fort Road, the coast road from Gosport to Lee-on-the-Solent.

R.H.C. Ubsdell, Alverstoke, 1841. On the otherside of the wall is Church Road
(PMRS 1945/419/2)

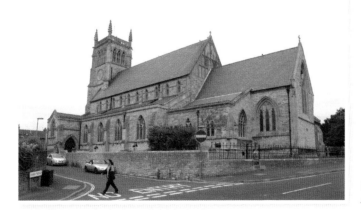

St. Mary's frontage to Church Road
Anglesey Road in foreground

Crescent Road and Crescent Gardens
Angleseyville Alverstoke

The Anglesey Hotel

Owen had been commissioned by Robert Cruickshank, an entrepreneurial Gosport solicitor. Cruickshank's other projects included the first Haslar toll bridge and the Floating Bridge ferry that linked Gosport to Portsmouth. For the Crescent, Cruickshank led a partnership including Owen's father that used their connections to the Board of Ordnance to acquire land overlooking Stokes Bay. Their intention was to develop the resort of Anglesey Ville to exploit the fashion for sea bathing that had developed in the reign of George III and for a number of years their resort was very popular. Owen planned a double crescent, but only the first crescent was built. At the end of this block is the Anglesey Hotel. This would originally have been in the centre of the crescents and would have looked over the classically designed Reading Room with its Ionic columns and its two flanking bath house pavilions where residents could bathe in cold or warm sea water. On either side of the Reading Room were the Crescent Gardens to which the residents of the Crescent would have a key and which turned the curved form of the Crescent back into a rectangle. The back edge of the gardens ended in The Terrace Walk from which the shipping in the Solent could be viewed. Sir Charles Austen was at one time a resident of No. 2 The Crescent. The Reading Room and Bath Houses are gone but the hotel and gardens have been lovingly restored and are open to all. The hotel serves excellent food and has a friendly bar. Cruickshank persuaded Bishop Sumner that St Mary's would not be able to cope with the residents of his new town and possibly Owen's obvious patching-up of St. Mary's and Ubsdell's watercolour were part of this process! Thus St Mark's Church opposite to the Crescent mews opened as a Chapel of Ease, but a clear rival to St Mary's, in 1844.

Doubtless this led to the re-building programme at St Mary's and the ultimate demolition of St Mark's in 1911. The churchyard of St Mark's is lovingly maintained by volunteers and remains the resting place of many distinguished army and navy officers.

St Mary's Chancel and nave were rebuilt in 1863, and in 1881 the Nave was heightened, clerestoried and the roof extended over the remains of the tower. The tower and its roofed extension was then demolished in 1904 and funds raised to build the present imposing tower.

The churchyard has over 500 gravestones some dating from 1666 onwards, many of the graves are of distinguished sailors. G.M. Bligh is buried near the Lych Gate, a young officer on H.M.S. Victory at Trafalgar and whose home for some time was Blighmont, Millbrook, Southampton.

Ubsdell's watercolour of 1841 has the same date that Samuel Wilberforce, the son of William Wilberforce and cousin to Charles Richard Sumner Bishop of Winchester (1827-1869), became Rector. He was to hold the post until 1846. He was also chaplain to Prince Albert and founded the first two National Schools for young children. He later became Bishop of Oxford before succeeding his cousin as Bishop of Winchester. Ubsdell probably obtained the image of Samuel Wilberforce, that was later to appear in his composition 'Sermon at St Lawrence Ventnor IOW April 1844' at the same time the watercolour was completed.

Between 1809 and 1825 the Rev. Charles A. North had been Rector; the son of Bishop Brownlow North, Bishop of Winchester, and Lord of the Manor of Gosport. Charles North was a close friend of Ubsdell's mentor John Christian Schetky, and whilst teaching at the Royal Naval College in Portsmouth periodically used to live with Charles North's family at Alverstoke rectory.

Schetky's daughter tells in her biography of her father how the two met. Schetky was lodging in Oxford and happened to look out of his window and saw a large setter dog fall from a two storey window of the Angel Hotel opposite. Schetky ran to the street and obtaining cord and wooden splints from an upholsterer's shop bound up the dog's broken leg. The owner came to the street and Schetky laid into him for his cruelty in throwing the dog from the window, but the owner explained that it had been the dog's mistake, as it was used to the broad window ledges of the Bishop of Winchester's Palace at Farnham. Schetky and Charles North were friends from that day.

R.H.C. Ubsdell, Rowner, St. Mary The Virgin 1841 (Southeast side)
(PMRS 1945/419/50)

Rowner, St. Mary The Virgin
(Southeast side)

The Churches at Rowner and Titchfield served the Gosport peninsula until Alverstoke church was built in the 12th century.

Rowner offers the chance to look from a beautiful old chapel dating from the 12th century straight into a wonderful 20th century auditorium and vice-versa. Off the auditorium are meeting rooms offering community facilities, a coffee shop, a slimming club, a youth club and mother and toddler sessions.

Ubsdell's painted two watercolours of Rowner in 1841. In one view the church is seen with the conventional orientation with the tower being in the west, followed by the 12th century nave and the smaller 13th

Rowner St. Mary the Virgin

century chancel, and a similar offset projection of a later chantry chapel for the Brune family who held the lordship of the manor.

Ubsdell also painted the church from the North and in this view we see the 2 windows of the west wall, the chantry chapel, and the 13th century sanctuary joining it to the nave.

The church underwent a restoration in 1874 and further work between 1884 and 1919 which were clearly extensive but which left the essence of the church unchanged. In 1968 the West wall was removed and a huge modern extension built, but this was destroyed by fire in May 1990. The present magnificent steel, glass and wood auditorium replaced the previous extension in 1992.

R.H.C. Ubsdell, Rowner, St. Mary The Virgin 1841 (Northwest side)
(PMRS 1945/419/51)

Rowner, St. Mary The Virgin
(Northwest side)

Whilst many churches have modern extensions, it is perhaps the dramatic way in which the beautiful old building compliments the beautiful new building that is particularly striking.

Looking from new to old

Looking from old to new

The church has a memorial to The Reverend Charles Brune Henville. M.A. 'Successively fellow of New College Oxon and St. Mary College Winton whose remains are interred with those of his brother in the same vault. He was for many years the zealous incumbent of Portsmouth and Portsea and afterwards vicar of Hound and Bursledon and perpetual curate of Hamble where he died on the 17th of July 1849 aged 68. This monument was erected in testimony of their esteem and gratitude by M.J. Player, E.I. Brigstocke, William, James and Philip Thresher; Great Grandchildren of William Henville of Haydon'.

Ubsdell had been married by Charles Brune Henville, in 1833, and he encouraged Ubsdell by having a lithograph made of the inside of St Thomas's, and introduced Ubsdell to the Bishop of Winchester, Charles Richard Sumner, who subsequently commissioned and purchased many of Ubsdell's watercolours of churches.

Brune or Brun is a name very much associated with the church, as King Edward 1 granted the Manor of Rowner to Sir William le Brun in 1277, and two Brune sons, Philip and Nicholas were given the office of Rector between 1292 and 1306. The Brune family sold the last of their

The Rev. Charles Brune Henville
(Hampshire Records Office)

Rowner estate for housing in 1948 but still retain the Lordship of the Manor of Rowner. Richard Prideaux-Brune is the current patron of the benefice and appoints the rector, continuing a seven centuries long tradition.

The church website highlights that in the chantry is a rare solid limestone sepulchre tomb to Sir John Brune, Lord Chancellor of England, who died in 1559, and is one of two such structures in the country. Its escutcheons reveal the careful marrying that went on to secure the family's wealth, linking with de la Rokele, Bamfilde, Ticheborne and Knowles.

Crofton St. Edmund's

R.H.C. Ubsdell, St. Edmund's Lychgate Green, 1841
(PMRS 1945/419/15)

The church that Ubsdell painted is now dedicated to St. Edmund and survives at Lychgate Green, Crofton and is cared for by the Friends of Crofton Old Church. Pevsner describes it as 'an accumulation of homely architecture of several centuries', a 15th century nave, the chancel and the little S. chapel 14th century, a west wall of Georgian brick and a big S. transept of the early 19th century'. The scalloped front wall shown in Ubsdell's picture has however been replaced by a more conventional triangular aspect.

As the village of Stubbington expanded a new church was built there called Holy Rood in 1878, with a church tower being added in 1928. A fire at the chancel end led to a refurbishment in 1968 with an impressive church centre being added in 1991.

Stubbington, Holy Rood 1878

Crofton, St.Edmund's Lychgate Green PO14 3HA

Fareham S. S. Peter and Paul

Fareham SS. Peter & Paul 1742
Tower and 1931 Nave

Of the church shown in Ubsdell's watercolour of 1841 only the lady chapel, and the tower exist today, the latter being built to replace an earlier tower and steeple in 1742. The lady chapel is at the far end of the church as you come in through the new porch.

It was here the church guide tells us that 'the Great Seal of England was exchanged on 2nd July, 1346 at the command of King Edward the Third, before his expedition left for France and the Battle of Crecy. John de Oford, the Chancellor, delivered the Great Seal to be used during the King's presence in the realm, to John de Thoresby, before the High Altar, and received from him the seal to be used during the King's absence'.

Ubsdell's watercolour shows the 1814 nave that replaced its Medieval predecessor, this was 'built of local brick with round headed windows of the plainest design, factory like in appearance and meanly built. The porch at the north entrance was added in 1822...The nave was eventually reconstructed to a design by Sir Charles Nicholson completed in 1931'.

The chancel meanwhile had been rebuilt in 1888 to a grand design by Sir Arthur Blomfield for the reconstruction of the whole church, but only the chancel, choir vestry and south transept (built to house the organ) were ever built.

R.H.C. Ubsdell, Fareham SS. Peter & Paul, 1841
(PMRS 1945/419/19)

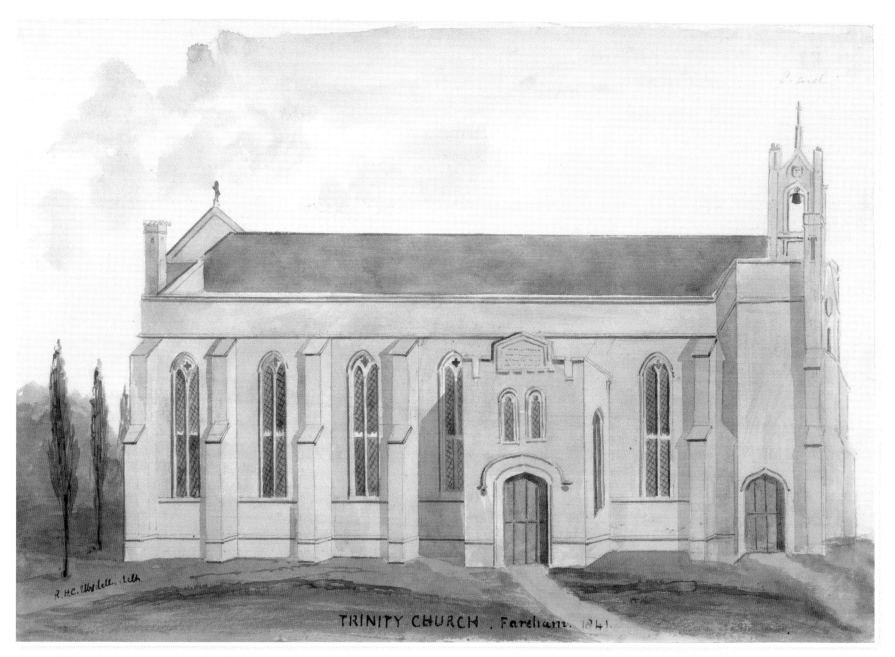

TRINITY CHURCH . Fareham. 1841.

R.H.C. Ubsdell, Fareham Holy Trinty Church, 1841
(PMRS 1945/419/20)

Holy Trinty today

Holy Trinty today from the gallery (above) and (right) view from the east end.

There is something about Ubsdell's watercolours of Holy Trinity, Fareham, of St. Paul's Sarisbury Green and of St. James East Tisted that is very geometric and created with the aid of a ruler rather than freehand. Also they are very similar to what was built, but certainly not, exactly what was built. The first two are known to be churches by Portsmouth architect Thomas Ellis Owen. East Tisted is not known to be by Owen, but the 1839 parsonage that stands between the church and the road is by him. This suggests that with these churches Ubsdell worked from the architect's drawings rather than from life. The common link between Ubsdell and Owen is the Portsmouth & Portsea Literary & Philosophical Society. Owen designed their building that opened on 29th June 1829 and was situated between the current Highbury and King Charles Streets in Portsmouth. Owen was a frequent lecturer on architectural topics to the society, as was Ubsdell on art. One of Ubsdell's two main patrons was the Bishop of Winchester, who was very critical of the quality of Owen's designs. This may be because many of Owen's churches were funded by the Treasury under the 1818 Church Building Act, which aimed to provide worship for the maximum number of people for the smallest cost, with the objective of trying to forestall the kind of revolutionary uprising seen in France. Maybe this is why some of Owen's churches such as the second St Mary's in Portsmouth did not stand the test of time? Perhaps these Ubsdell watercolours were artist's impressions and designed to commend the look of these buildings to the Bishop and other interested parties?

Holy Trinity is a simple but very beautiful church with an iron frame and attractive painted cast iron columns, and slender beams running across a flat ceiling. The frame is faced with yellow brick and stone. The church was built in 1834/5 and its construction was partly funded by its first rector the Reverend Sir Henry Thompson in memory of his mother. Thompson was the son of Jane Dame Thompson and Vice Admiral Sir Charles Thompson Bart who was second in command under Sir John Jervis at the battle of Cape St. Vincent.

Bishop Charles Richard Sumner consecrated the church for divine worship on Thursday 3rd December 1835.

Ubsdell's watercolour is from 1841, the year before the delicate tower was removed and replaced with a square buttressed tower, to house a clock and a larger tenor bell. A slender spire was added in 1847 but this had to be removed in 1992 due to its deterioration. Side galleries were added in 1836 but were removed in the next century. The original church had no chancel. A whole new east end was added in the 1920s to house the altar and the original east window was moved to the west end.

The Rev. Sir Henry Thompson Bart also built the school room cum chapel at Funtley.

Portchester Castle

The Keep of Portchester Castle

Probably in his late teens, like his brothers, fellow artist Dan, and hairdresser William Chinn, Ubsdell had spent some time in London getting more experience of his trade. John Christian Schetky could have introduced him to Clarkson Stanfield, who at this time would have been working on huge diorama stage productions. At Drury Lane for a Christmas production they had a moving transparency, 700 feet of translucent painted calico 20 feet high illuminated by gas light gradually wound from reel to reel, taking the audience on a twenty minute journey by day and night to the falls of Niagara. He may even have met Louis Daguerre who had invented the Diorama and was working on a method of making them easier to reproduce by capturing images directly from nature by coating the calico with silver iodide and exposing it to the scene that needed to be reproduced.

Doubtless inspired by the Great Exhibition in London in 1851 and 1852 Ubsdell was the artistic mastermind behind turning the keep of Porchester Castle into a theatre. The side walls were decorated with similar designs to those he had helped create in 1842 for the purpose of decorating public buildings in England and France to celebrate the new Entente Cordiale. The remains of these can still be seen today. A viewing platform in wood similar to today's steel and glass would have been created and the audience would look down on an illuminated diorama and magic lantern show on the far wall.

Portsmouth Harbour from the roof of Portchester Keep Roof, Horsea Island to the left

On 19th July 1851 the Hampshire Telegraph talked of 'the Mammoth Picture of Vesuvius, by Ubsdell: the ERUPTION of the MOUNTAIN, allowed to be the chef d'oeuvre of Pyrotechny'. A more splendid show followed the next year as reported in The Hampshire Telegraph for 27th March 1852:-

'A Magnificent Panorama of Iceland;- Exhibited in Colossal dimensions, and many thousand feet of canvas being covered by the pencil of the artist, (and some novel mechanical contrivances, having been brought into requisition) MOUNT HECLA and the Yokuls and other Craters, with their numerous volcanic Mountains, and Geysers, or boiling fountains, emitting volumes of steam and spouts of boiling water…. As dusk approaches, REINDEER and HERDSMEN will be seen crossing the numerous Bridges over the Falls, and leading homeward various sounds attributable to volcanic action begin to strike the ear. As night comes on flashes of fire will be seen issuing from the summit of the mountain this will be signal for the portending Eruption. Columns of fire with loud reports of cannon fall in quick succession, the western side of the Mountain is rent from top to bottom, LIQUID LAVA and Stones roll down and choke up the valleys, CATARACTS of FIRE destroy and consume all this by day appeared so fair, and thus in DARKNESS and apparent DESOLATION is ended this magnificent specimen of artistic talent and skill.'

Perhaps the previous year's performance didn't go quite that well, as the Hampshire Telegraph went on to say;-

'In the production of the above combination of the work of the Artist's pencil and mechanical contrivance and skill, the proprietors have spared no expense, taught by the experience of the past season they have succeeded in avoiding the many crudities and imperfections incidental to a first attempt of such a character, and the result of a liberal though wise employment of capital, experience, and skill, is the production of a work of art of a character and magnitude never attempted before in the provinces'.

Ubsdell's decoration of the side of the theatre

Modern version of the theatre
upper viewing platform

(English Heritage, Stephen Conlin)

Hamble-le-Rice waterfront

Warsash Ferry Jetty Hamble-le-Rice waterfront

AIRCRAFT SITES

1) FAIREY AVIATION (1915)
2) ADMIRALTY SEAPLANE DEPOT NOW OIL TERMINAL
3) VARIOUS SITES USED OVER THE YEARS BY AVRO SOUTH AERODROME AND FACTORY J. D. SIDDELEY OF ARMSTRONG WHITWORTH AIRCRAFT, FOLLAND AIRCRAFT, HAWKER SIDDELEY, SMITHS AEROSPACE, GENERAL ELECTRIC.
4) AVRO NORTH AIRFIELD J. D. SIDDELEY AIRSERVICE TRAINING FOR CIVIL AND MILITARY PILOTS.

MARINAS

A) HAMBLE POINT MARINA
B) PORT HAMBLE MARINA
C) MERCURY YATCH HARBOUR
D) ELEPHANT BOATYARD
E) SWANWICK MARINA

As regards the church of Hamble St. Andrew Pevsner comments that much of the church is Norman including the tower with frequent re-using of parts. Externally the church seems very similar to the watercolour Ubsdell painted in 1841.

The River Hamble was once navigable as far as Botley forever associated with the radical politician William Cobbett author of 'Rural Rides' an invaluable account of the English countryside in the early 19th century in the aftermath of the French Revolutionary and Napoleonic wars.

For me raised on the visions conjured up in the 1980s serial 'Howard's Way' the Hamble is a bit disappointing. It is just too crowded with boats and boatyards and has little to offer the casual tourist. You really need your own boat and crew, preferably with a pontoon in Port Hamble Marina, (the one closest to the village), or are a member of one of the Hamble Village yacht clubs. Possibly Cowes or Gosport have more to offer?

Hamble has a proud aviation history that started with its attraction of its Solent frontage for the manufacturers of seaplanes. Hamble had a vital role in WW2 for aircraft maintenance, repair and conversion, and being so near to Spitfire production at Woolston, Southampton, and Chandler's Ford, Eastleigh was mainly responsible for keeping that fighter flying. The defunct northern aerodrome, an area of land that still exists between the eastern and western approach roads to the village played an important role in pilot training before and after the war. It is a shame that more is not made of this. The only clue is the red Folland Gnat T Mk 1 of 1960 vintage that stands sentinel by the sports ground and Kings Avenue access road to GE Aviation the remaining aerospace parts manufacturer at Hamble.

The Bugle Hamble

Gnat T Mk 1 manufactured by the Folland Aircraft Company in 1960 marks the entrance road to the aircraft parts factory at Hamble now part of GE Aviation

La Dolce Vita Hamble

Hamble ST. ANDREW

Ubsdell had known Charles Brune Henville as vicar of Portsmouth, but in 1838 he became instead the incumbent of the first three River Hamble churches. He was perpetual curate of Hamble, and the vicar of Hound and Bursledon. Possibly Ubsdell painted these churches to gain the interest of Henville, and through Henville the introduction to the Bishop of Winchester, Charles Richard Sumner?

R.H.C. Ubsdell, Hamble-le-Rice St. Andrew's, 1841
(PMRS 1945/419/29)

Hamble-le-Rice St. Andrew's

St Mary's is on Hound Road the first turn left when coming from Hamble having passed over the railway. The first road on the left after the church gives foot access to the Royal Victoria Country Park on the site of Netley Hospital virtually all demolished in 1966 apart from its chapel which is now the visitors' centre. Construction of the military hospital commenced in 1856 as a reaction to the terrible hospital conditions experienced in the Crimean War. The hospital was grand but impractical being over a quarter of a mile long, The hospital was criticised by Florence Nightingale for its lack of ventilation and for not being of her preferred design of multiple ward pavilions open on three sides, running off a wide central corridor. The hospital had its own jetty into Southampton Water and its own rail connection.

This old rail connection is now part of a circular walk, the 'Hamble Rail Trail'. Parking near the Country Park tea rooms you can follow the line of the old hospital rail connection up to the main line, then follow a footpath and the actual rail track of the WW1 branch line connection to the gates of the site of the old Admiralty seaplane depot, now a BP fuel depot. From here you can cross Hamble Common down to the Solent Way footpath and back to the Country Park. The rail connection is no longer used as BP built a pipeline connecting their Wytch Farm oil field in Dorset to the Depot. Much of the track has not been lifted as the rail link might still be useful for bringing crude oil from newly discovered small oil fields to the depot.

The church of Hound, St Mary's was built around 1230 by the Benedictine monks of the nearby Priory of Hamble-le-Rice, only the bell turret (late 15th century) and the vestry (1922) are older. Restorations over the years have left the church looking very much Ubsdell's watercolour of August 1841.

R.H.C. Ubsdell, Hound Church, 1841
(PMRS 1945/419/37)

Hound St. Mary's

Netley Abbey

A little further along Southampton Water is Netley Abbey a large open space with romantic ruins to explore. It is the most complete surviving monastery in southern England. When the monasteries were suppressed, Henry VIII granted Netley to Sir William Paulet in 1536 who then transformed the buildings into a great Tudor courtyard house. In 1704 the house was sold for building materials, but demolition stopped when a construction worker was killed. The ruins became overgrown and writers and artists were attracted to the atmospheric ruins including Thomas Gray, Horace Walpole, John Constable and Jane Austen. In the 1840s, as now, it became a popular place for local people to come for tea, dancing and music. At some stage however the overgrowth was cleared and the Tudor alterations were removed. Ubsdell's watercolour then is particularly interesting as the ruins depicted do not relate to anything remaining today.

Netley Abbey

R.H.C. Ubsdell, Netley Abbey, 1841
(PMRS 1945/419/42)

Bursledon ST. LEONARD'S CHURCH

Like Hound, Bursledon was founded by Benedictine monks, but slightly earlier in 1109. In 1391, overseas (particularly French) priories were seized by the crown, and Hound and Bursledon were given to Winchester College so it could benefit from the tithe income in return for providing clergy. Ubsdell's watercolour shows the transepts added in the 1830s. The architect Sedding however rebuilt the transepts in 1888-9 and extended the nave and tower forward into the bank, nearly up to the point where the men sit on the tomb in Ubsdell's painting.

R.H.C. Ubsdell, Bursledon, St. Leonard's
(PMRS 1945/419/8)

Bursledon St. Leonard

THE ELEPHANT BOATYARD

Parking is limited in Bursledon, so arriving by boat, foot, or train may be a good idea. The Jolly Sailor is a pub worth visiting, as is the Ferry Restaurant in The Elephant Boatyard. This is located in one of the passenger sides of the old chain link ferry that used to shuttle between Southampton and Woolston before the Northam bridge was built. The 'Floating Bridge' that used to carry passengers and cars from the end of Broad Street in Old Portsmouth to Gosport was similar, and Ubsdell would have been a frequent passenger. The present Elephant Boatyard is on the site of the historic boatyard of the same name that built Lord Nelson's flagship at the battle of Copenhagen. It also stood-in as Jack Rolfe's Mermaid Boatyard that Tom Howard invested his aerospace redundancy money into, in the BBC's hit 1980s series Howards' Way.

The Ferry Restaurant in the Elephant Boatyard

The River Hamble from the end of Lands End Road

THE STEAM BRICKWORKS

A fascinating attraction open a restricted number of times a year is the Bursledon Steam Brickworks. Southern Hampshire had numerous brickworks, as the Eocene clays found here are particularly suitable for brick making. Bursledon was founded in 1897 by Mr Ashby and was latterly owned by the Redland Brick Company. The M27 cut the site in two and half the site was then sold to form Swanwick Nature Reserve and the air traffic conrol centre, whilst the old buildings were sold to Hampshire Buildings Preservation Trust, who have gradually restored them, and the historic machinery they contain. There is also a comprehensive exhibition of building materials and methods.

Sarisbury Green St. Paul's

R.H.C. Ubsdell, Sarisbury Green, 1842
(The Dean and Chapter of Winchester Cathedral)

St Paul's was originally a chapel of ease within Titchfield Parish and was built on land known as Titchfield Common gifted to the Ecclesiastical Commissioners by the Lord of the Manor, Henry Peter Delmé. The church was officially designed by Southampton architect George Guillaume, although it may have been based on Thomas Ellis Owen's original rejected plans. Owen is said to have surveyed the completed building. The church was erected in 1835 and Ubsdell's watercolour was painted 7 years later in 1842. The real church looks more substantial than the drawing, and the real colours seem much more muted. Of course the little church has been expanded considerably over the years. In 1880 a chancel and sanctuary were added on the east end of the building and in 1908 an enlarged vestry and organ chamber were added and a lych gate.

A clock was mounted in the western face of the bell tower in 1877 and an additional five memorial bells were installed in the bell tower in 1815. A memorial chapel was built on the south side of the church in 1921, a reading room was added circa 1870 and in 1891 a parish room and a large school room were built onto the existing reading room. The later additions probably made the church function a lot better, but maybe they have detracted from the simple beauty of the original plan.

The east end of St. Paul's with all its additions

Sarisbury Green St. Paul's

Sarisbury Green interior

Botley & Durley

BOTLEY

At one time the Hamble was navigable as far as Botley. Botley will be forever associated with William Cobbett (1763-1835) a radical politician, when criticising the establishment could be highly dangerous. He spent 2 years in jail between 1810 and 1812 for speaking against the use of flogging in the army. He was most famous for his book Rural Rides.

The modernised stable block of Cobbett's Botley House now called Cobbett's House.

Durley, Holy Cross

DURLEY HOLY CROSS

Not far from the source of the Hamble is Durley.

Durley Holy Cross dates back to sometime between 1270 and 1284. Gilbert White the celebrated Selborne naturalist became curate of Durley in September 1753, and held the post for eighteen months. Ubsdell's watercolour was completed in Jan 1842. Externally the church is little different from Ubsdell's painting, although the yew in front of the south transept has now grown so massive that it is impossible to replicate Ubsdell's viewpoint.

R.H.C. Ubsdell, Durley Holy Cross,
Jan 1842
(PMRS 1945/419/17)

KEY

1   Cowes Castle

2   St. Mary's Church, West Cowes

3   Northwood House & Park

4   East Cowes Castle

5   Norris Castle

6   St. John The Baptist Church, Northwood

7   Sts. Thomas Church, Newport

8   The River Medina Basin, Newport

9,10,11   The Isle of Wight Steam Railway
         Wootton Station, Haven Street Station
         and Smallbrook Junction Station

Cowes: The view from Northwood Park over Cowes Castle the home
of the Royal Yatch Squadron, looking towards Lee-on-the-Solent

Isle of Wight

The places Ubsdell chose to paint on the Isle of Wight were connected to the portraits of the people he also painted. Many of the originals of these portraits are lost, but many of their images survive in Ubsdell's composition 'Sermon at St Lawrence Ventnor IOW April 1844' (see page 28). Undoubtedly Ubsdell would have known John Christian Schetky, a keen sailor who had briefly sailed with the legendary Thomas Cochrane. Schetky was teacher of drawing at The Royal Naval College Portsmouth from 1811 to 1836, and held various appointments as a painter of marine subjects in the courts of George IV, William IV and Queen Victoria.

Most importantly, Schetky was an honorary member of the Royal Yacht Squadron. He was not a noted portrait painter, but he was loved for the way in which he assisted his pupils and his fellow artists. He would be more than likely to recommend Ubsdell for portrait work, and it is probable that through Schetky Ubsdell gained introductions to the enthusiastic amateur sailors and their naval honorary member colleagues, who formed the Royal Yacht Squadron. Members would have included The Earl of Yarborough, the first Commodore of the club, The Duke of Rutland, Lord Hardwicke (whose local

seat was Sydney Lodge on the Netley Road Hamble) and, if not formally members, the illegitimate sons of William IV by his mistress Mrs Jordan; Lord Adolphus FitzClarence, (who commanded the Royal Yacht) and Lord Frederick Fitzclarence (who was Governor of Portsmouth). Ernst Leopold, 4th Prince of Leiningen was an honorable member from May 1859. He had joined the Royal Navy in 1849 and commanded the Royal Yacht in the 1860's.

The Yacht Club had been founded in 1815, with the Prince Regent joining in 1817. It added 'Royal' to its name in 1820, before becoming the Squadron in 1833. It moved into its impressive base in Cowes Castle in 1858.

The 1937 Fifth Edition O.S. map is particuly interesting as it shows the full extent of George Ward's Northwood Estate at West Cowes, John Nash's East Cowes Castle, and Norris Castle built by architect James Wyatt for Lord Henry Seymour.

Queen Victoria and Prince Albert bought Osborne House in October 1845 together with Barton Manor to house the equerries and grooms. The architect was Thomas Cubbit who also designed Kings Cross Station. Building took place between 1845 and 1851.

West Cowes St. Mary's

R.H.C. Ubsdell, West Cowes, St. Mary's 1845
(The Dean and Chapter of Winchester Cathedral)

Until the 19th Century Cowes was part of the parish of Northwood and it was not until 1894 that the parishes of St Mary's Cowes, and St. John the Baptist Northwood became separate entities.

Ubsdell's watercolour of 1845 shows St. Mary's with its tower erected in 1815 by George Ward to house pews for his family, and with a burial vault for them beneath. The tower was designed by John Nash and in the background can be seen Northwood House, George Ward's mansion. The chapel had obviously grown over the years, extended eastward in 1811, and with the small chancel in the picture added in 1833. On 2nd May 1867 Miss Emma and Miss Charlotte Ward, daughters of George Ward laid the foundation stone of a new church, with a new lofty nave with clerestory windows that reached far higher up the existing tower. On either side of the nave the aisles contained large balconies. Despite the enlargement, the church retained much of the look of its predecessor. A vestry was added in 1893, and the chancel was extended in 1900.

St. Mary's as rebuilt in 1867, 1893 and 1900

Interior of St. Mary's

Northwood Park

The 'Nunnery Steps' at the top of Castle Hill. At one time an underground passage ran from here to the cellars of Northwood House.

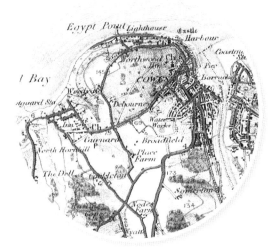

George Ward (1751-1829) was a prominent City banker and a director of the huge East India Docks in London. He was encouraged to come to the IOW by William Arnold, the Collector of Customs and father of Dr Thomas Arnold the pioneering headmaster of Rugby School. Ward bought a house called Bellevue and with the assistance of John Nash the prominent Regency architect turned it into the grand Northwood House between 1798 and 1802.

Nash undertook the enlargement of Buckingham Palace, and for himself built a picturesque castle at East Cowes on the other side of the River Medina. The latter is no longer in existence, although some of its stone was used in extensions at the R.Y.C.'s Cowes Castle.

George Ward's son, George Henry Ward (1784-1849) extended the house further with a new western wing and an entrance pavilion on the north side of the house. Dying without an heir, the estate went to George Ward's second eldest son, William Ward (1787-1849) MP, director of the Bank of England, gentleman cricketer and saviour of Lords cricket ground. On William's death the estate was inherited by his son Dr William George Ward, (1812-1882) a prominent theologian who converted to Roman Catholicism. Whether Ubsdell painted the portraits of these gentlemen or other members of the Ward family one cannot say, but the presence of Northwood House in the background of St Mary's Church means he almost certainly tried!

In 1929, Captain Herbert Joseph Ward gifted Northwood House to Cowes Urban District Council.

Northwood House as extended by George Henry Ward

Northwood ST. JOHN THE BAPTIST

St. John The Baptist, Northwood, dates from the 12th Century, with most of the major work being done in the 15th Century. Some time after a print dated 1794 a wooden bell tower was removed and a stone tower constructed together with the short steeple shown in Ubsdell's watercolour.

St John the Baptist, Northwood

Ubsdell's first known painting on the Isle of Wight was the church of St John the Baptist, Northwood, painted in the bleak winter of 1840/41. This church with origins in the 12th century, was the daughter church to Carisbrooke, and was in turn the mother church to the West Cowes Chappell that had begun as a Puritan Meeting House in 1657. It seems likely that the church at Northwood was painted at the same time as Ubsdell had come to the island to paint a miniature of the Earl of Yarborough.

R.H.C. Ubsdell, St John the Baptist Northwood, 1841
(PMRS 1945/419/44)

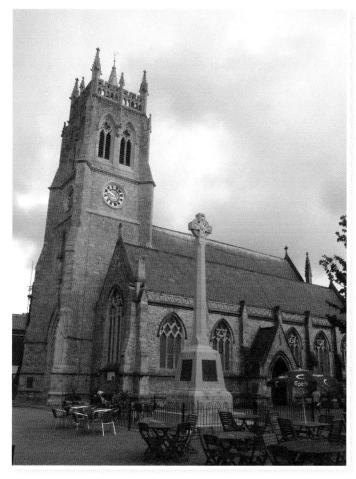

Newport Parish Church 1854

Newport STS. THOMAS

Newport was a major junction for the railways but now the railways here are no more and a new road runs where once the trains crossed the River Medina.

RIVER MEDINA, NEWPORT LOOKING UPSTREAM

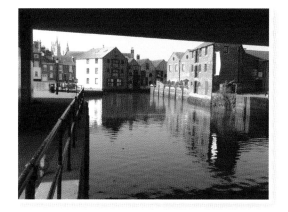

nk

RIVER MEDINA, NEWPORT LOOKING DOWNSTREAM

Newport's Parish Church, Sts. Thomas was rebuilt in 1854. Ubsdell had painted the West End of the previous church and the East doorway in 1842 but the whereabouts of these watercolours is unknown. The new church does however contain many artefacts from the previous church including the fine alabaster and marble tomb of Sir Edward de Horsey, Governor of the Isle of Wight from 1565 until 1582.

Isle of Wight Steam Railway

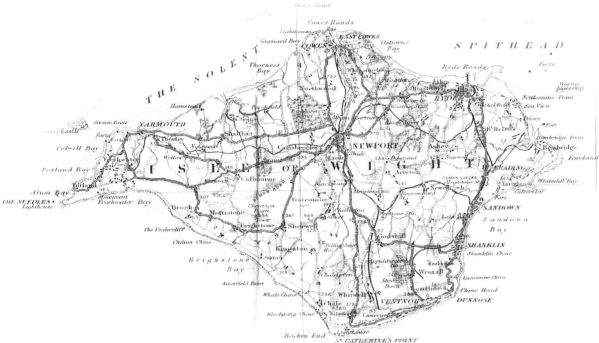

The railways came late to the Isle of Wight, the line between Cowes and Newport in 1862, Ryde & Shanklin in 1864, Shanklin to Ventnor in 1866, between Ryde and Newport in 1875, Sandown to Merstone in 1879, Brading to Bembridge in 1882, between Newport and Freshwater in 1889, and Newport to St Lawrence and through to Ventnor Town in 1900. Today only Ryde to Shanklin remains operated by ex-London Transport tube stock and The Isle of Wight Steam Railway from Smallbrook Junction to Wootton. Many of the disused railway lines are now cycle paths including Newport to Sandown (Perowne Way), Newport to Cowes, Wooton to Newport, and Brading to Bembridge.

The Isle of Wight Steam Railway is special because of the age of its rolling stock and is as close an experience as it is possible to get to Ubsdell's journey by train to Winchfield and home by way of Winchester, that he undertook in 1845.

Ventnor

R.H.C. Ubsdell, Crab and Lobster, Ventnor, 1843
(PMRS 1945/419/62)

In 1843 Ubsdell with money in his pocket from painting members of the French Court, took a holiday and stayed at the Crab & Lobster Inn, Ventnor, Isle of Wight. The Inn is still there although now it is holiday accommodation. The inn got replaced by the King Charles 1 Hotel, that in turn became apartments, whilst the hotel's stables became the new inn:- the Crab & Lobster Tap.

Whilst at Ventnor Ubsdell would have recorded the interior and exterior of the church at St Lawrence and planned how he would recreate his images of the principal members of the French and British Courts all sat round in the smallest Parish Church in England.

Landlords Simon and Victoria Woods outside
The Crab and Lobster Tap

The Crab and Lobster, now holiday appartments

Ventnor

Appuldurcombe

Appuldurcombe House

Stone Fountain Basin installed by the Earl of Yarborough, looking towards Wroxall

The bell at St. Lawrence Church originally at Appuldurcombe House

Certainly at some time, Ubsdell painted the face of the Earl of Yarborough, for it was to appear later in 'Sermon at St Lawrence', the picture in which the famous people he had painted are all seen sitting round in reputedly the smallest parish church in the country, and the church for which Yarborough in his nearby mansion of Appuldurcombe was patron. Yarborough sits on the extreme right of the picture. Fellow Royal Yacht Squadron member Charles Yorke, 4th Earl of Hardwicke sits beside him. The painting is Ubsdell's 'masterpiece'. It was created as an advertisement for his skills, and as a conversation piece to be put on display in his art gallery and studio. Ubsdell specifically names Yarborough on the back of the canvas. The painting would lose its essential point if the people in it, and especially the Earl, had not all been previously painted by him.

The Yarborough miniature was probably painted to fulfil a wish of the Royal Yacht Squadron to have a portrait of their founder. The miniature, would then most probably have been sent to London where the fashionable London studio of Henry Perronet Briggs R.A. would have set up a dummy appropriately clothed, and from the face and the clothed dummy, produced the full length portrait that hangs at Cowes Castle today. From the Briggs portrait, George Raphael Ward produced a Mezzotint published on the 8th May 1841.

The first meeting of the Yacht Club that would eventually become the Royal Yacht Squadron was held at the Thatched House public house in London on 1st June 1815.

Founder members included the Hon Charles Pelham, the future Earl of Yarborough, who would be appointed the first Commodore in 1825 and William Baring (1780-1820) the 4th son of Sir Francis Baring and uncle of Francis Baring the Whig politician M.P. for Portsmouth from 1826 to 1865. Also present at that first meeting and relevant to our story were the Rev. Charles North, son of Bishop Brownlow North and friend of Ubsdell's mentor John Christian Schetky, and The Earl of Uxbridge shortly to lose his leg at Waterloo and acquire the title of first Marquis of Anglesey, and have a development on the Gosport peninsula named after him.

Of the Marquis of Anglesey the first history of the squadron relates that:

'Lord Anglesey was very proud of the whiteness of the decks of his famous cutter, the Pearl, and when he gave a passage to Lord Adolphus Fitzclarence, who wore carefully varnished boots which left marks on the deck after a shower, he told off one of the hands to follow the offender with a swab and remove the mark of each footstep.' Lord Adolphus Fitzclarence would later be the subject of a lithograph based on an Ubsdell painting. [*1]

Charles Yorke, 4th Earl of Hardwick who sits next to the Earl of Yarborough in 'Sermon at St. Lawrence' succeeded to his title 18th Nov 1834 and was a life-long friend of John Christian Schetky, who was his drawing master at the Royal Naval College. Hardwick was elected to the Squadron in 1847. Together with the 5th Duke of Rutland they formed a close friendship circle in old age. Hardwick had an extensive naval career:

'When in command of the Vengeance man-of-war at Genoa in 1849, during the Piedmontese war with Austria, he took all the English residents aboard and refused to move his ship, although the republican commander sent a message to say that if he did not the guns of the batteries would open fire and sink her. Lord Hardwick himself led the landing party which brought away the refugees, and was met by an infuriated mob prepared to attack him. On getting out of the boat he walked alone towards them, and seeing a woman advancing ahead of the rest with a very furious aspect, he coolly took her by the arm and kissed her. The people were so captivated by his readiness and presence of mind that they cheered him heartily, and

he brought away his countrymen without difficulty. Lord Hardwicke was a familiar figure at Cowes in later years, and was known to his intimates as "Old Blowhard". [*2]

When Sir Robert Peel and the Conservatives came to power in September 1841, Lord Hardwicke was appointed as one of the Lords in Waiting to Her Majesty and acted as ambassador to the King of Prussia early in 1842 and to the Emperor of Russia in the summer of 1844.

Hardwick on the introduction of Schetky probably gave Ubsdell access to Queen Victoria's Court, and thus he would have obtained the images of the people in his painting of Queen Victoria meeting the Corporation of Portsmouth, destroyed by German bombing of Portsmouth in WW2.

The Earl of Hardwicke

Archdeacon Samuel Wilberforce

Charles Cecil Cope Jenkinson 3rd Earl of Liverpool

Lady Emma Lascelles, Baroness Portman

Queen Victoria

Prince Albert

There are images of the above in existence at different stages in their lives, but Ubsdell's images would appear to be unique. His miniatures of the Earl of Liverpool and Lady Portman was exhibited at The Royal Academy in 1845.

Queen Victoria and Prince Albert probably didn't sit for him. Fortunately Ubsdell's visit to Court coincided with the first visit to England of celebrated painter of the French and European Courts Franz Xaver Winterhalter. Winterhalter probably provided Ubsdell with images of the Queen, & Prince Albert & Edward Prince of Wales, and quite possibly a recommendation to the French Court by which means the images of Prince Louis-Philippe Albert d'Orleans and his mother The Duchess D'Orleans were obtained.

[*1] p. 46 The Royal Yacht Squadron Memorials of Its Members
[*2] Ibid, p. 207

St Lawerence

R.H.C. Ubsdell, Sermon at St Lawrence Church, Ventnor IOW. April 1844.
Comprised of images of the famous people Ubsdell had painted as minatures.

The Church at St Lawrence

Before the addition of the chancel in 1830 the church was only 25 feet long and 11 feet wide and was considered the smallest parish church in England. Ubsdell therefore chose to sit his celebrated sitters in a celebrated 'box' that would hold them neatly.

Interior of St Lawrence

Churchyard and church today

Portsdown Ridge and Coastal

Seaward Side

One of the most puzzling of Ubsdell's watercolours is the view across fields up to Nelson's Monument, a column 120 feet tall, standing high on Portsdown Ridge. The monument dates from 1807, two years after Nelson's death at Trafalgar. In Ubsdell's picture the monument stands straight ahead and a little to the left of the viewer. No water separates the viewer from the monument, so the viewpoint has to be from the meadows that lie below Portchester Castle. Today the view is very different. The monument is completely hidden by trees and it is only from the roof of Porchester Castle itself that the very tip of the column can be seen.

Porchester Ridge became of great defensive importance in the 1860s when with the development of muzzle loading artillery with rifled barrels, and the explosive shells to go in them, it was realised that Portsmouth might be vulnerable to an attack from inland, and thus a number of massive red brick forts were built. From the West, these were Fort Wallington, Fort Nelson, Fort Southwick, Fort Widley, Fort Purbrook, and the Farlington Redoubt.

R.H.C. Ubsdell, Nelson's Monument Portsdown Ridge circa 1841 (PMRS 1945/419/47)

Nelson's Monument from the roof of Portchester Castle

Much of the ridge became MOD property and thus research facilities filled vacant space between Forts Nelson & Southwick and Forts Southwick & Widley, the Eastern end of this block resembling the tower and radar dome of a Class 47 destroyer. The far Eastern end of the ridge is occupied by Camp Down, before the modern London Road, the A3 (M), crosses under the ridge road and descends the hill to the Farlington Marshes. This was the site of a semaphore station used by the Navy to send messages between Portsmouth and London before the electric telegraph was invented. Today Fort Nelson is part of the Royal Armouries, a museum dedicated to telling the story of artillery through the ages. Fort Southwick is storage space awaiting redevelopment, its car park used as a Park & Ride by staff working in the giant Queen Alexandra hospital that lies on the ridge flank beneath. Forts Widley and Purbrook are now Peter Ashley Activity centres, named after the Portsmouth councillor that set up the charity that runs them. Widley hosts equestrian activities and Purbrook is a large camp site available for hire for a wide range of sporting and leisure activities, The Farlington Redoubt has been demolished.

In the present day view of Nelson's monument Fort Nelson can just be seen behind the fourth pylon from the left whilst the course of the M27 lies in cutting running across the picture behind the line of roofs furthest up the hill.

Whilst the seaward side of the ridge is no longer rural the views from the top are spectacular, and the countryside that lies behind a delight of country lanes, small villages, and country pubs.

Nelson's Monument

Fort Purbrook

From Nelson's Monument looking over Portchester Castle to the Spinnaker Tower on Gunwharf Quays Portsmouth

CONSECRATED
TO THE MEMORY OF
LORD VISCOUNT NELSON
AND THOSE WHO FOUGHT AT
TRAFALGAR
TO PERPETUATE HIS TRIUMPH
AND THEIR REGRET
MDCCCV

The Landward side of Portsdown Ridge is a world of woods, of winding roads, a different world to the hustle and bustle of Portsmouth and the M27 east-west corridor. Boarhunt, Southwick, Denmead, Hambledon and the remains of the Forest of Bere await you.

R.H.C. Ubsdell, Boarhunt St Nicholas, July 1841
(P.MRS 1945/419/6)

Boarhunt St. Nicholas

Southwick St. James and Priory

R.H.C. Ubsdell, Southwick St James July 18th 1841 (PMRS 1945/419/57

Southwick St James

Southwick Priory was founded by Henry 1 in 1133 in the church of St Mary Portchester, within the walls of Portchester Castle, but moved to the site at Southwick a few years later. Under the Dissolution of the Monasteries the priory was suppressed, the surrender being signed on 7th April 1538. At its height the Priory had acquired at least 18 manors, other lands and rents, and 5 rectories including those on Portsea Island. Thomas Wryotheslye (pronounced Risley, 'fixer' to Henry VIII, see Titchfield page 108-111 acquired vast estates during the Dissolution, including the Priory and the manors of Southwick and Boarhunt with which he rewarded his servant, John Whyte. John Whyte converted the Prior's lodgings into a private house. This burnt down in 1750, and its replacement in 1841. The present Southwick House was built on the site and was part of HMS Dryad, the School of Maritime Operations until 2004. In the following year it became the Defence College of Policing and Personnel Administration, uniting the police training facilities of the three Services. It later took the title 'Defence College of Policing and Guarding'. Whyte pulled down the Priory itself, but a piece of wall remained that Ubsdell painted in 1845 and which remains to this day in the South West corner of the old estate, next to the golf course. During World War II Southwick House became the Supreme Headquarters Allied Expeditionary Force (SHAEF) under the Supreme Commander General Dwight D. Eisenhower.

R.H.C. Ubsdell, The remains of Southwick Priory 1845 (PMRS 1945/419/58)

The remains of Southwick Priory

Sir Francis Austen's Widley and Wymmering

Widley and Wymmering play a significant part in the Jane Austen legend because Portsdown Lodge was the home of Jane's brother Admiral Sir Francis William Austen GCB, from when he bought the estate in 1828, with the assistance of Mrs Leigh Perrot, until his death in 1865. Portsdown Lodge occupied the westwards corner between the Ridge Road and the road to Waterlooville that was the old London Road. On the eastwards corner was The George, a coaching inn where teams of horses would be changed having toiled up the hill from Portsmouth. The estate was aquired by the military when the Portsdown forts were built and the highest part of the estate was taken for a water reservoir at the end of the 19th Century. Plots facing the London Road and bottom part of the estate were sold for housing. A number of oaks stood at the top of the ridge and marked the Portsmouth boundary. Every year there used to be a 'beating the bounds' ceremony, and Boundary Oak School occupied the Portsdown Lodge building until it too was sold for development in 1961. The Garden Dell (probably a small chalk quarry) is now the location of Dell Close. In Sir Francis's day there would have been a magnificent view of Portsmouth from the top of the ridge, and views across to Southwick, Denmead and Hambledon.

R.H.C. Ubsdell, Wymmering Church 1842
(PMRS 1945/419/76)

Wymmering Church

Site of Portsdown Lodge

Rear of Portsdown Lodge

Dell Close

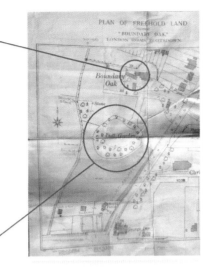

Front of Portsdown Lodge

Jane Austen's two youngest brothers were Francis and Charles, both of whom were educated at the Royal Naval College Portsmouth and joined the Navy. Francis was the elder of the two. Ubsdell painted a miniature of Jane Anna Elizabeth Lefroy nee Austen, Jane's niece and daughter of eldest brother James. Portraits of Francis and Charles are probably also by Ubsdell. Jane's beloved sister Cassandra died at Portsdown Lodge March 22nd 1845. Sir Francis was not there however, having been called back to active service on The Vindictive 5 days earlier. Cassandra was Jane's literary executor, and after Cassandra's death Anna Lefroy inherited the manuscript for Jane's last and unfinished novel 'Sanditon' and was left with the conundrum of whether to publish the fragment as it was, or attempt a continuation and completion of the story. Anna did attempt a continuation, which was itself unfinished. The fragment of Sanditon was published in 1925 and Anna's continuation in America in 1983.

The original St Mary Magdalene Widley Church was adjacent to Mill Farm on Widley Walk but was finally demolished in 1953. It was probably unsafe through most of the 1840's, was rebuilt in 1850 but then its village was moved East to the other side of the London Road so as not to give cover to an enemy trying to attack Fort Widley from inland. This left the troops who manned Fort Widley and Fort Purbrook without a church and so Christ Church Portsdown was constructed in 1871 and consecrated in 1874. The army financed the land and was given the right to hold military services in the church, and to use the churchyard for military burials. There is an extensive graveyard of mainly WW1 graves to the rear of the plot.

A vigil was held at the church prior to D-Day.

Sir Francis Austen's church was therefore Wymmering, (nowadays spelt with one 'm') which lies in 'old' Wymmering just south of the modern A3. Jane Austen, mother Cassandra, sister Cassandra, James Austen's wife Mary and close friend of the family Martha Lloyd lived with Sir Francis's Family in a big house in Castle Square Southampton between 1806 and 1808 following the death of Jane's father in Bath, and before moving to Chawton. Francis's first wife died after the birth of her 11th child in 1823 and Martha Lloyd became his second wife in 1828. Martha died at Portsdown Lodge in 1843. Her large stone monument and headstone in the front corner of the churchyard flanks that of Francis's daughter Cassandra Eliza who died unmarried age 35 in 1849. Francis himself has a small stone on the other side of the path and a brass memorial by the Lady Chapel altar.

Graves of Cassandra Eliza and Martha Austen

Sir Francis Austen's Grave

Wymmering Manor, dating back to 1581, and in urgent need of renovation, lies on the other side of Old Wymmering Lane, just North of the church. Between 1804 and 1813 its notable occupants were Harris Bigg-Wither, his wife Anne Howe Frith, and their family. Harris's call to fame was his accepted proposal to Jane Austen in 1802. Unfortunately for him Jane retracted her acceptance the following morning.

The oldest part of Wymmering Church is the North Arcade with its round Norman arches dating from around 1180 AD. The south Arcade with its pointed Early English arches followed in around 1220 AD and the Chancel around 1400AD. A singing gallery and a battlemented belltower were added in the 18th Century. Ubsdell painted the church in 1842 but like many others he recorded at that time, it was damp and in poor condition. Wymmering was one of the first churches in the district to be re-worked by George Edmund Street in 1861 with considerable rebuilding of floors and walls, a new vestry, south porch, and new bell tower.

R.H.C. Ubsdell, Storm over Wymmering
(PMRS 1945/419/77)

Edward Mogg The Road from Bath to Brighton 1817

R.H.C. Ubsdell, Volunteer Review Portsdown Ridge 1868
(PMRS 1986/98)

The scene is of the eastern end of Portsdown Ridge viewed from fields to the east of Cosham, to the south of Drayton and just north of Farlington Station. Fort Purbrook can be seen on the ridge to the left of the picture and Farlington Redoubt can just be seen towards the right of the picture on the ridge before it descends down to Bedhampton. Farlington village can just be made out below Farlington Redoubt.

The forts had been designed to prevent an attack from inland, but to avoid compensating private landowners, it was decided that an enemy had landed in Sussex and had somehow managed to silence the forts and occupy the ridge. A force of volunteers therefore threw two pontoon bridges across Hilsea Channel and a flotilla of gunboats and steam launches advanced up Portchester Creek and bombarded the right flank of the enemy in the vicinity of Paulsgrove. The main battle however was for the village of Cosham to which the invaders were driven, and forced to retreat up the hill, their flank being contained by the forces seen in the picture which advanced up the London Road to hold the eastern side of the ridge.

R.H.C. Ubsdell, Farlington St Peter July 1841
(PMRS 1945/419/21)

Farlington St. Peter's is thought to date from 1104 and Bedhampton from 1132. Both churches were in a poor condition by the middle of the 19th Century and under the direction of architect G. E. Street both were rebuilt, Bedhampton in 1868, Farlington's new chancel in 1872, and its new nave in 1875. Bedhampton was extended to the North in 1878 with a further extension for a new parish room, vestry, kitchen, and toilets in 1993.

R.H.C. Ubsdell, Bedhampton
St Thomas à Becket 1841
(PMRS 1945/419/3)

Bedhampton St. Thomas à Becket

Havant is dedicated to the child martyr Faith, tortured by Dioclecian under Dacian, Governor of Spain circa AD 303. The church was enlarged and rebuilt following the previous pattern between 1832 and 1875.

R.H.C. Ubsdell, Havant, St. Faith 1841
(PMRS 1945/419/32)

Havant St. Faith

Warblington St. Thomas à Becket

R.H.C. Ubsdell, Warbington St. Thomas à Becket circa 1841
(PMRS 1945/419/63)

Today, Warblington lives in its own little world cut off from Havant by the A27(T), and has to be approached by car from the southern roundabout after the slip roads leading to Emsworth, although pedestrians and cyclists can still gain access by means of the delightfully named Pook Lane. To the east of Warblington Church it is less than a mile down the Church Path to Emsworth. This path forms part of both the Solent Way and the Wayfarer's Walk.

In Roman times a villa stood to the north east of the church and after the Romans left, Saxons established the village of Weorbel's people, Weorblington in around A.D. 50. A monastery and church were established on the site between 959 and 975 A.D. The centre portion of the Saxon tower dates from this time, but was rebuilt between 1290 and 1340, and a new nave constructed towards the road. The chancel was then rebuilt on the foundations of the old church and a chapel, now the vestry, added on the north side.

In 1340 the north porch was added containing a number of ships' timbers from the 14th Century.

The Manor of Emsworth was split from that of Warblington sometime in the 14th Century but both populations were then decimated by the Black Death of 1348. Warblington became the possession of Richard Neville, Earl of Warwick who turned the area around the Manor House into a deer park. Consequently, when populations recovered settlement was at Emsworth, or nearer to Havant. In 1515 Margaret Countess of Salisbury built a large castle on the site of the old Manor House and Henry VIII visited in 1526, King Edward VI in 1552, and Queen Elizabeth in 1586. Today only a single turret stands from the original gateway, as the then owning family, the Cottons, had supported the Crown in the Civil War, and their castle had been besieged and reduced by Parliamentary forces.

The church underwent further improvements in the 19th Century. Ubsdell's picture shows the addition of the spire, but the trefoil window high up in the West wall had yet to be added, and the outside steps up to a door which presumably led to an internal balcony had yet to be removed. The Church underwent restoration in 2011 following an electrical fire that destroyed two pews and created considerable smoke damage.

North Porch

Warbington St. Thomas à Becket

Emsworth is a pretty waterside town famous for its grain mills and oysters. South Street leads down to a dock and slipway. To east and west of the town there are the tidal mill ponds. The eastern pond is fed by the River Ems and powered the Slipper Mill. Below it was a further mill pond, now the marina, that originally powered the Lower Slipper Mill. The western pond was fed by the West Brook and powered Quay Mill, now the home of the sailing club.

Both mill ponds were allowed to fill with water on the high tide, and the head of water in the pond powered the mill as the tide fell. A lock gate at Quay Mill, allowed boats into the pond with the tide. A promenade was built around the western pond in the 1920s that makes a very pleasant walk. Much of the harbour estuary was given over to oyster beds and a flourishing fishing and trading industry ran from Emsworth of boats dredging the Channel for oysters and scallops. However the growing population of Emsworth led to pollution and deaths from typhoid and the sale of Emsworth oysters was banned in 1903. A sewage treatment works was finally completed in 1914.

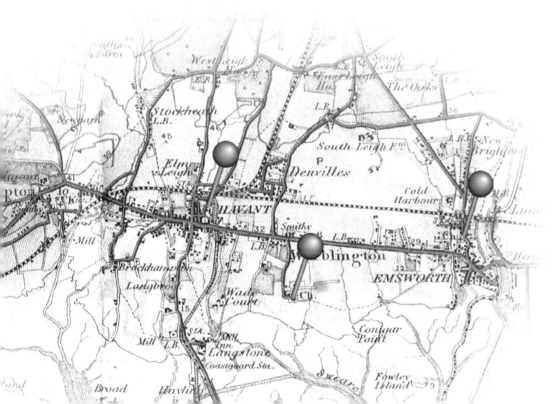

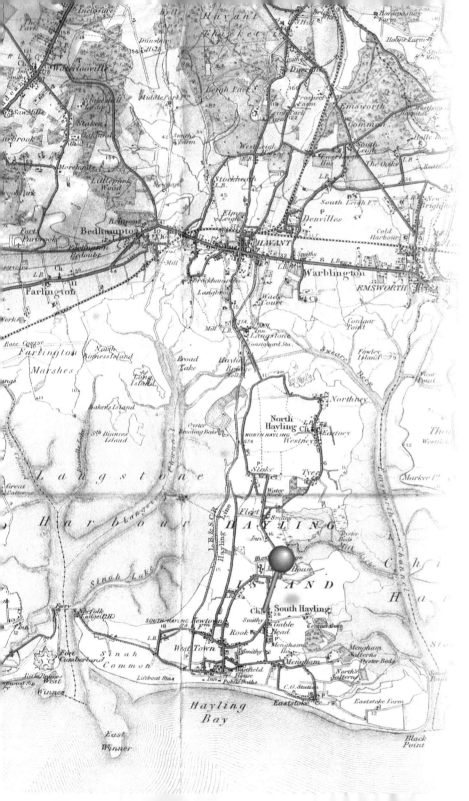

Hayling Island

(P.Hocquard/www.transporttreasury.co.uk)

Hayling Island lies to the east of Portsea Island on the other side of Langstone Harbour. Hayling is reached by a road bridge from Havant to the north, whilst Emsworth lies to the north east. A railway branch line used to run over a trestle bridge parallel to the road bridge, but the line closed in 1963. The trestle bridge was a wonderful setting for photographs of the diminutive 'Terrier' tank engines that hauled a couple of ancient coaches along the line, mainly for the benefit of holidaymakers. Today similar engines and coaches form most of trains on the Isle of Wight Steam Railway (see page 84) and the route of the old railway forms a cycle path all the way back to Havant. In the summer there is a foot passenger ferry to Eastney on Portsea Island. The main attraction of Hayling Island is the three mile long beach looking out over the Solent. The beach is sandy below the high water line. The West end of the beach is shallow, sheltered and warms quickly as it is protected by a sandbank to the west.

South Hayling ST. MARY'S

South Hayling, St.Mary's

Ubsdell painted St Mary's South Hayling in July 1841. St Mary's has a considerable history and certainly met Ubsdell's criteria of paintng the most ancient and curious churches he could find. A large part of Hayling Island was submerged in 1324 and again in 1340 and the first church 'All Saints' was lost to the sea at that time, although the font survives in the present church which dates from 1253. St Mary's today is much as Ubsdell painted it. The octagonal spire clad with oak shingles is clearly recognisable, although struck by lightning in 1872, damaged in the great storm of 1887, and hit by lightning again in 1999. The giant yew is even more massive.

The South Porch constructed around 1400 of oak on a stone base, looks much the same, although repaired in 1893, and again in 1916, as it had started to fall forward. In Ubsdell's day the floor was medieval stone sepulchral slabs, but the floor was tiled in the 1860's. South Hayling has a particularly large porch. In medieval times the first part of baptism and marriage ceremonies took place there, and seats were provided as it was sometimes also used as a school or a place of business.

South Hayling, St. Mary's July 1841
(PMRS 1945/419/34)

South Hayling Porch July 1841
(PMRS 1945/419/35)

South Hayling Porch

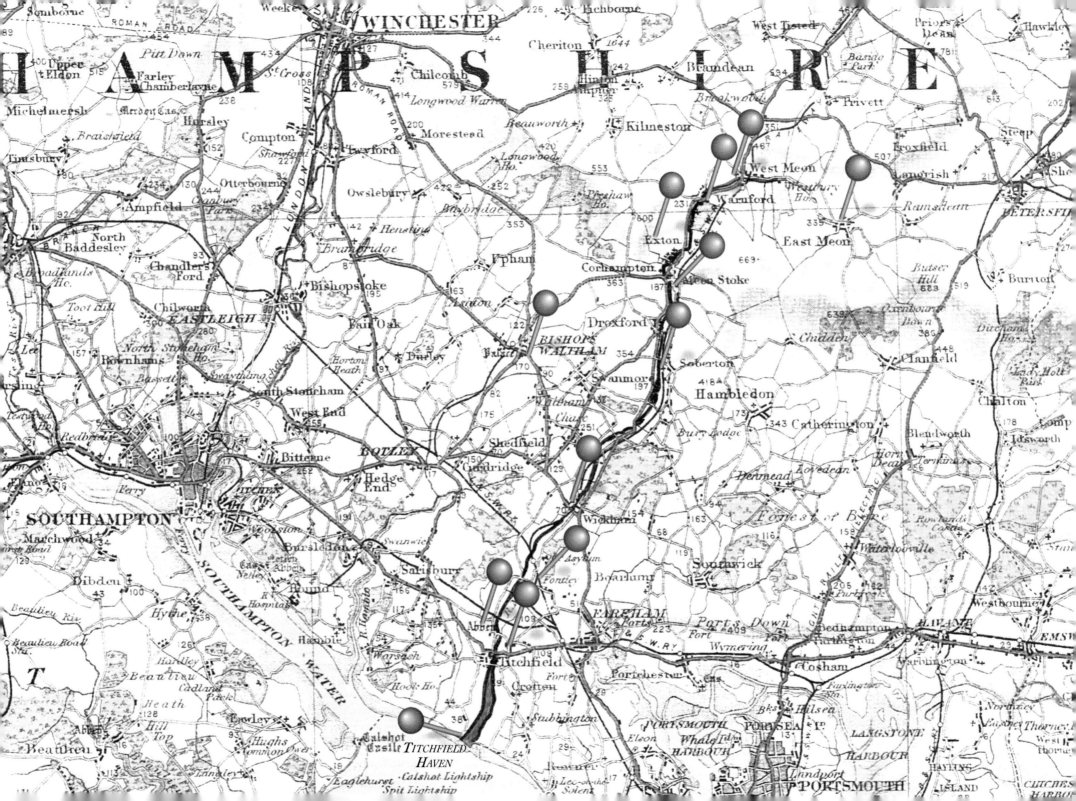

Titchfield Haven

The Meon Valley

The Meon Valley cycle trail between Wickham and West Meon gives wonderful access to this beautiful valley.

River Meon, Hillhead Harbour & Titchfield Haven

Hillhead Harbour

If you follow the coast from Gosport, heading towards Southampton you pass through the beach-side town of Lee-on-the-Solent, before climbing onto a stretch of cliff with its commanding views of The Solent. You descend the cliff to find yourself in the valley of the River Meon. The river no longer makes its way to the sea by means of its natural estuary because of works undertaken between 1594 and 1611 by Henry Wryotheslye the third Earl of Southampton. The monument to his grandfather, the first Earl, Thomas Wryotheslye, his wife Jane Cheney, and only surviving son Henry the second Earl is, as we will see, in St Peter's Church in Titchfield. The third Earl married Mary Browne, daughter of the 1st Viscount Montagu and is famous for being a patron of Shakespeare and for being an active member of The Virginia Company and its colony at Jamestown.

The third Earl built a sea wall across the mouth of the Meon with a sluice that allowed some water flow into Hillhead Harbour and the passage of migratory fish. Alongside the River Meon he built a canal as far as Titchfield, entrance to which could be achieved at high tide by means of a sea lock. The coast road turns inland heading towards Titchfield and narrowing to just two metres, passes over a three-arched stone bridge in the position of the previous inner lock gate.

The tow-path of the canal remains and makes a pleasant walk from Hillhead Harbour to meadow immediately below St. Peter's Church Titchfield which in earlier times was the site of a substantial dock and leather tannery.

The Earl's scheme included the reclamation of the marshes alongside the river. Today there is hardly any water in the old canal, and the water level in the old river estuary is maintained at a height to make it an attractive wetland for birds. Titchfield Haven is a National Nature Reserve with an attractive visitor centre run by Hampshire County Council.

The Titchfield estates had belonged to Premonstratensian Abbey of Titchfield, but Wryotheslye acquired the Abbey and the estates in 1537. The Abbey he turned into Place House and in front of the centre of the old Nave of the Abbey he built a grand turreted gatehouse. Much of Place House was allowed to become a picturesque ruin in 1781, but what remains is in the care of English Heritage. The Abbey can be found on the banks of the Meon just north of Titchfield on Funtley Lane, that leads you to Funtley and on to Wickham.

In 1741 Peter Delmé bought the manor of Titchfield including Titchfield Haven. When the Delmé male heirs died out the estate passed to the descendants of two co-heiresses: Elizabeth wife of the Rev. Charles Delmé Radcliffe, and Julia married to Captain James Arthur Murray R.N.: respectively Colonel Emilius Charles Delmé Radcliffe, and George Delmé Murray, the latter living at Place House.

This book is about Ubsdell's paintings and their connections. I bought one of his paintings on EBay for £100, Fair Rosamond. It illustrates 'The Ballad of Fair Rosamond' by Thomas Delone published in London in 1612, which tells of King Henry II's love for his mistress following their meeting in 1166. She was Rosamond Clifford (< 1150 – c. 1176) and possibly died at the hands of Henry's queen, Eleanor of Aquitaine. The alternative version of history is that Henry's liaison with Rosamond became public knowledge in 1174 and ended when she retired to the nunnery at Godstow near Oxford in 1176 shortly before her death.

The Ballad tells that Henry installed Rosamond at a hunting lodge at Woodstock. The lodge was in a forest and its entrance was protected by a labyrinth. However the end of a silk thread had fallen from a needlework chest that the King had given to Rosamond, and following this thread Eleanor was able to find Rosamond's bower and contrive her death by the dagger or poison, by accusing her of the sin against God of adultery.

Woodstock Palace and the hunting lodge were later demolished and replaced by Blenheim Palace.

Charles Dickens tells the story of Fair Rosamond in his 'Child's History of England' written between 1851 and 1853.

Fair Rosamond already an engraving by William Blake was a popular subject with the Pre-Raphaelites and their followers. Arthur Hughes and William Bell Scott painted the subject in 1854, Frederick Sandys in 1858, Dante Gabriel Rossetti in 1861, Edward Burne-Jones in 1862. Later there are notable pictures by F.W. Waterhouse and Frederick Cowper.

For Ubsdell, 1866 saw him at the height of his success living in the big house at 1 Green Row and with a successful photographic studio, and a growing reputation. Doubtless his "Fair Rosamond" was an attempt to be compared with the best. His picture shows Rosamond at prayer asking God for forgiveness for her sins and deciding whether to drink the poison. Queen Eleanor towers over her, the thread she has followed in a purse hanging from her waist, poison in one hand, dagger in the other, her guards looking on, uncertain how to resolve this confrontation between wife and mistress.

The inscription on a label on the original back-board of the painting reads '..painted by R.H.C. Ubsdell Portsmouth 1866 for F P Delmé Radcliffe Esquire of Hitchin Priory'. Frederick Peter had been a captain in the Grenadier Guards, was a notable sportsman, Master of the Hertfordshire Hounds, and would on occasions have hunted with the Hambledon pack. He was author of 'The Noble Science: a few general ideas on Fox Hunting' a work with illustrations based on original designs by his brother, the Rev. Charles Delmé Radcliffe (1806-1865). The work went through 4 editions and became a sporting classic. Frederick had a number of sons. Son, Frederick Peter was killed in the Crimea in 1854, and Seymour Walter in India in 1860. Sons, Commodore Francis Augustus Delmé and the Reverend Arthur Henry Delmé Radcliffe however survived their father who died in November 1875.

How the painting came into being must always remain a mystery, but it seems like another example of Ubsdell's sense of humour. Delmé Radcliffe was a member of the Royal Yacht Squadron and he had a ketch called Fair Rosamond!

Fair Rosamond 1866

Titchfield St. Peter's – The First of the Meon Valley Churches

The Meon Valley acts as a barrier preventing the conurbation of Portsmouth, Gosport and Fareham from completely merging with Southampton and its suburbs. Titchfield, as the first village you meet as you travel north from the mouth of the River Meon, manages to keep its identity. Many of the houses are centuries old. I stayed in a cottage where its floors were made from uneven chunks of old wooden battleships, hauled up the river, or their dismembered parts brought up the later canal. Its High Street is an ancient square with the bow windows of the Bugle Inn adding interest, but the effect is somewhat spoiled by the parked cars.

Titchfield High Street

In the churches of the Meon Valley a booklet is on sale entitled 'In the Steps of Saint Wilfred The Meon Valley Pilgrimage Trail'. Produced by the Revd Jim Foley in 2005 it aims to tell people about the spiritual history of the valley, interesting facts about the churches, and a suggested route to walk from one church to another.

The Romans had left in the year 411, and from 466 the Meon Valley began to be populated by pagan-worshiping Saxons and Jutes, the Meonwara. Bishop Wilfrid sailed up the River Meon as far as Titchfield in 681 and began to convert the Meonwara to Christianity, a process that lasted until the year 686. He built the predecessors of the churches we see today. A row of Roman tiles in the porch at Titchfield and characteristic limestone blocks date from the original 7th Century building. Exton was built in 940, but the church at Corhampton is unique in that the stone building that replaced the wooden structure in 1013 has remained virtually the same ever since. Some of these churches are truly ancient. It was this aspect of the churches that attracted Ubsdell and the patrons of his watercolours.

Ubsdell painted Tichfield in 1840 and most of the rest of the churches in the August of 1841, although Soberton and East Meon are notable absentees. He began painting the exteriors of churches after a chance meeting with Sir Frederic Madden (1801-1873) at Titchfield St. Peter's. Madden was Keeper of Manuscripts at The British Museum. He had been born in Portsmouth and remained fascinated by its past, and planned to write a history of the town. Ubsdell hoped to illustrate this work. Between 1839 and 1857 Ubsdell wrote frequently to Madden suggesting new subjects from him to illustrate.

After their meeting at Titchfield Ubsdell wrote to Madden on Sept 18th 1839 seeking a commission to copy the Wryotheslye (pronouned Risley) family tomb. This two tiered monument in marble and alabaster commemorates the 1st Earl of Southampton, his wife and surviving son (d. 1550, 1574 and 1581) and is the work of Gerard Johnson a refugee from Flanders.

'The price of a drawing of this monument, finished on the spot, color'd from nature showing the chapel, banner, helmet, sword, gauntlet, would be 3 guineas. A sketch of the monument color'd £1-10-0. Beside the monumental effigies I find other subjects which I think would be an acquisition to your folio, if you have not seen them already. Place House, a beautiful ruin, a drawing of which would be 1 guinea. The picture about 14 inches by 12, a slighter sketch half a guinea. The picturesque stables commonly called Kg. Charles' stables belonging to the house would also make a fine drawing, price 1 guinea, or slighter sketch half a guinea. The view of Titchfield Church exterior makes a good drawing. I have already several commissions for the subject. If Sir F would like to see one of the drawings previous to giving a commission I could send one of monuments and one landscape view. I beg to say that I should like to exhibit a drawing of the monument next yr. All the drawings are to be carefully painted on the spot so I am engaged at Titchfield every week for some time.'

from B.L. Egerton Correspondence of Sir Frederick Madden Vol VI 1839-41

Ubsdell sent copies of the inscriptions and the heraldic shields to Madden together with his watercolour of the exterior of St. Peter's in October 1840. The whereabouts of the first items is unknown but the view of St Peter's from the east is in the Portsmouth Record Office collection.

Ubsdell tried very hard to emulate Madden as a learned academic and antiquarian, and thus he addressed The British Archaeological Association on the subject of the tomb in Titchfield Church.

'The monument has on it three figures, all as large as life; the countess is the shortest figure, being a lady. On the south side lies the chancellor Wryotheslye, Earl of Southampton.

The Wryotheslye Monument commissioned by Henry 3rd Earl of Southampton 1594 from Gerard Johnson the elder, a Flemish refugee

On the north side that of his son Henry. The tomb is not in a good state of preservation; it is so mutilated and injured as to grieve any one who views it.

On this (once) splendid monument are three shields at the west end, with supporters; and on the east end three inscriptions, with one shield of arms: one inscription to the chancellor, one to the countess, and one to Henry Earl of Southampton.

Four pillars are at the corners, which used to have ornaments gilded at the top — these are now gone; the banner of the Earl used to hang on the south wall of the chapel — this is now gone; the helmet and iron gloves were also there — they have been also removed. The banner was much torn and decayed when I copied it, about twelve years ago, and was hanging in silken rags. The three coronets are also much more damaged than when I made my first drawings of this work. I think some of the crests, black bulls coroneted, which were on litter shafts at the corners, are also missing; they are all loose.

Indeed, the whole monument requires restoration, and I assure you it is well worthy of it. On the sides of the tomb (south and north) are two kneeling figures, small, with altars before them, on which are books open. A small shield is in each compartment. I send you an engraving of the tomb (lately published in The Surplice) from a small drawing I made; but there is in the possession of Sir F. Madden, a most elaborate and careful drawing of the tomb;

also, all the shields of arms, rubbings of inscriptions, etc. This tomb has been opened of late years, and the coffins were all there; the hair was on one of the figures exceedingly perfect. All the figures and shields are coloured and gilt; and I think the restoration would cost but a trifle. I am not sure who are the descendants of the chancellor, but I think they should be applied to'.

Taken from the Journal - British Archaelogical Association "Proceedings of the Association" No.162 April 1842

Ubsdell's watercolour of St Peter's is seen from the paths that lead to the canal. Nearest to us is the 13th century chancel, remodelled in the 15th century. Ubsdell's picture shows us the original east window before it was replaced by the present 19th century Perpendicular version. On the far side of the chancel is the south chapel which houses the Wryotheslye monument. Ubsdell's picture also details the 15th century north aisle. The watercolour doesn't show the most striking feature of the church namely the tower, the bottom portion of which is 7th or 8th century and originally served as the west porch for an aisleless nave. The gates under the tower were made by the Third Earl's Funtley Ironworks in the 17th century.

*Wryotheslye's Place House
formerly Titchfield Abbey*

Titchfield St. Peter's

Titchfield St. Peter's tower

*R.H.C. Ubsdell, Titchfield St. Peter's 1840
(PMRS 1945/491/61)*

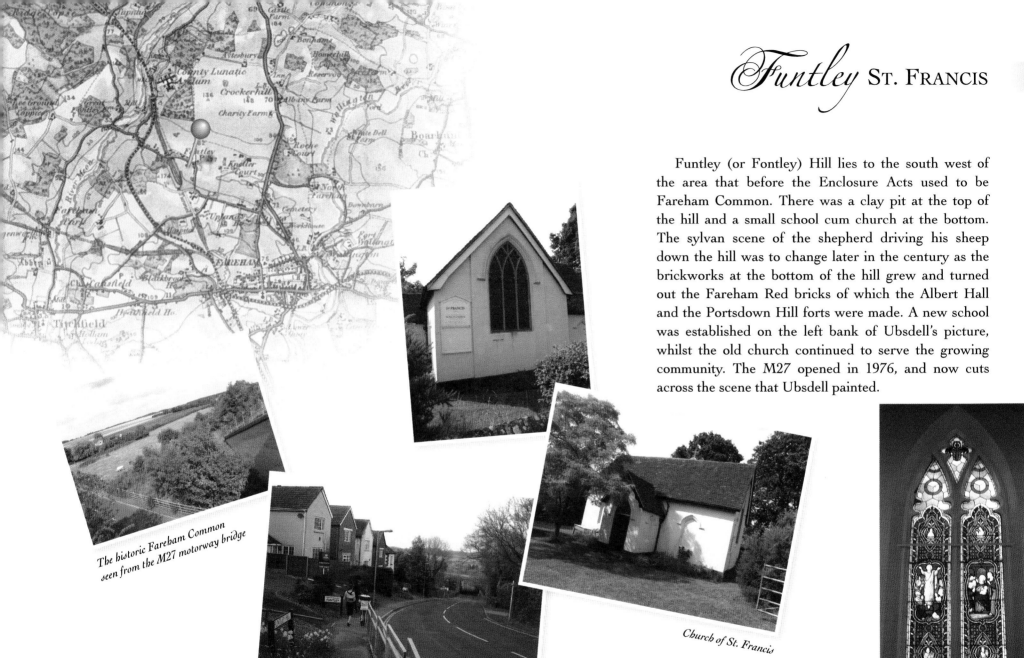

Funtley ST. FRANCIS

Funtley (or Fontley) Hill lies to the south west of the area that before the Enclosure Acts used to be Fareham Common. There was a clay pit at the top of the hill and a small school cum church at the bottom. The sylvan scene of the shepherd driving his sheep down the hill was to change later in the century as the brickworks at the bottom of the hill grew and turned out the Fareham Red bricks of which the Albert Hall and the Portsdown Hill forts were made. A new school was established on the left bank of Ubsdell's picture, whilst the old church continued to serve the growing community. The M27 opened in 1976, and now cuts across the scene that Ubsdell painted.

The historic Fareham Common seen from the M27 motorway bridge

Funtley Hill today

Church of St. Francis

Stained Glass Window designed by John Ruskin

FUNTLEY Church.

R.H.C. Ubsdell, *Church of St. Francis Funtley circa 1841*
(PMRS 1945/419/23)

Wickham St. Nicholas

Wickham St. Nicholas dates back to 1120 although it was almost entirely rebuilt in the 1870s. Much of the stonework was however sympathetically re-used, and the inside of the church is light and beautiful. Ubsdell's paintings do suggest a church in need of repair.

Wickham Church houses the monument to Sir William Uvedale (d 1616), Lord of the Manor of Wickham. Sir William is seen lying with his wife Mary, daughter of Sir Richard Norton of Tisted. Below them are their children; five girls and four boys. "Uvedale" is one of many ways to write in letters a name with a strong double "oo" sound as is 'übbsdell'. It seems possible that R.H.C. Ubsdell was a distant relation of Sir William Uvedale although the respective families probably branched sometime before 1475.

Wickham North Transept (foreground)

R.H.C. Ubsdell, Wickham North Transept (foreground) Aug 3rd 1841 (PMRS 1945/419/71)

R.H.C. Ubsdell, Wickham St. Nicolas Chancel (background) with South Transept (in foreground) (PMRS 1945/419/70)

St. Nicholas from the Meon Valley Railway cycle path

Sir William Uvedale Monument (D 1616)

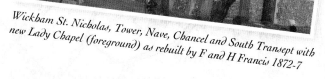

Wickham St. Nicholas, Tower, Nave, Chancel and South Transept with new Lady Chapel (foreground) as rebuilt by F and H Francis 1872-7

Tower and Nave (foreground) c.17th South Transept (background)

R.H.C. Ubsdell, Bishops Waltham, St. Peter's July 1841
(PMRS 1945/419/4)

'Waltham' means Settlement (Ham) in the Forest (Walt). 'Bishop' links the town to Bishop Henry de Blois, grandson of William The Conqueror, and brother of King Stephen and many subsequent Bishops of Winchester who were lords of the manor.

The present church dates from 1136. Ubsdell's painting of 1841 shows the west wall before it was in danger of collapse and had to be rebuilt in 1848 and the dormer windows replaced with windows 'of a more ecclesiastical character' twenty years later.

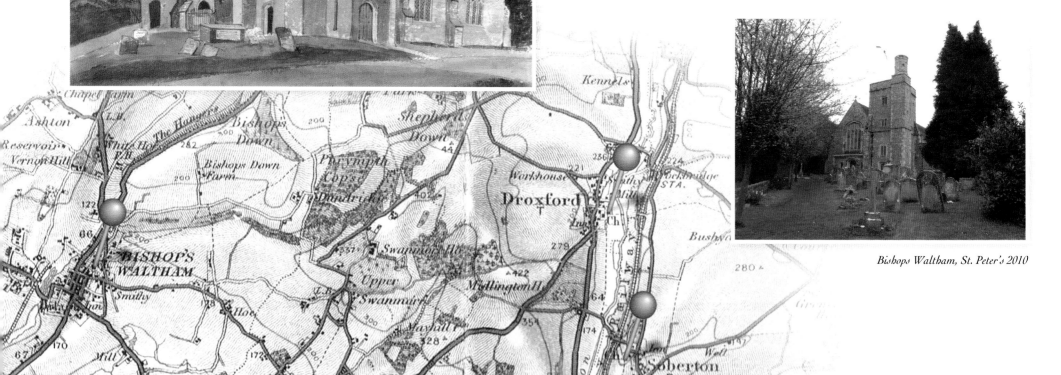

Bishops Waltham, St. Peter's 2010

Droxford St. Marys and All Saints and *Soberton* St. Peter's

A quintessentially English setting. Rectory, Manor House (pictured), Village Hall, churchyard, earliest parts of the church dating from 1150 to 1160. The original Norman part of the church is the central part of the nave denoted by the massive square pillars.

The South side of the church has the clerestory windows and the entrance doorway is Norman.

Most interestingly Ubsdell's view of the North side from August 3rd 1841 shows the heavily buttressed wall that would subsequently have been rebuilt and re-roofed.

R.H.C. Ubsdell, Droxford, St. Mary and All Saints 1841
(PMRS 1945/419/16)

Droxford

The River Meon on the road from Droxford to Soberton

Soberton St. Peter's (mainly 16th century)

I am indebted to the Rev. Jim Foley of Meonstoke, for his excellent explanation in his publication available for sale, price £4, in many of the churches in the Meon Valley, 'In the steps of Saint Wilfred, The Meon Valley Pilgrimage Trail'.

Meonstoke, St. Andrews 'was started in 1230 and local legend has it that it was built to rival Corhampton church, across the river, which was built in 1020. Apparently, the original inhabitants of Exton and Corhampton were Saxons and the Meonwara were Jutes and there was little love lost between the two tribes. Friction continued between the two communities for many centuries. A bridge was not built across the river until 1805 and as recently as the early 1900s a couple marrying from Exton and Meonstoke were cut off by their families; and the Rector's wife in the early 20th century refused to have anything to do with the people of Exton! So now there are two Anglican churches two hundred yards apart across the Meon.'

Of Meonstoke Jim Foley writes that; 'The tower was rebuilt of flint rubble in the fifteenth century and at that time the two side aisles would each have had their own separate roofs and the two quatrefoil clerestory windows which can be seen high in the nave would have been open to the sky. The church, which is rather dark now, would have been filled with light and colour in those days. The present roof covering nave and aisles was built in the eighteenth century. This necessitated raising the height of the nave roof by three and a half feet and the aisle walls by four inches. This, in its turn, left the tower dwarfed. Thus, the tower was given its present attractive and distinctive open top in 1909. The galleried wooden design was to save weight'.

Ubsdell's picture of 1841 is particularly interesting in that it shows dormer windows in the roof that would have let light into the quatrefoiled clerestories, and the tower before the 1909 alterations.

R.H.C. Ubsdell, Meonstoke, St. Andrew's Aug 1841
(PMRS 1945/419/39)

Meonstoke ST. ANDREW'S, *Corhampton and Exton* ST. PETER AND ST. PAUL

Corhampton church was built around 1020 in the time of King Canute on an artificial mound, possibly on the site of a heathen temple. It is a remarkable example of a pre-conquest church with windows inserted in the 13th century, that has otherwise remained largely unaltered. It is constructed of whole flints, plastered over, reinforced by stone quoins (corner stones), vertical pilaster strips or lesenes (columns) surmounted by a horizon string course of stone. The stone came from Binstead or Quarr on the Isle of Wight and shipped up the Meon. Ubsdell painted the surrounding churches of the Meon Valley in 1841. His picture would appear to show the east end, which originally had a round window, already re-built in red brick:- whilst existing authorities believe that the east end collapsed when the mound was cut into in 1842 for road construction. Ubsdell's painting also fails to show the enormous yew which today has a girth of 23 feet, so is around 1000 years old. The yew makes it impossible to photograph the same view as Ubsdell's watercolour where the yew is omitted!

R.H.C. Ubsdell, Corhampton (no known dedication) 1841
(PMRS 1945/419/14)

Saxon sundial that probably pre-dates the church

Corhampton interior

Corhampton 1000 year old yew
and rebuilt east end in red brick

Exton St. Peter and St. Paul

Exton Church dates from around AD 1230. It was largely rebuilt in 1847 and restored in 1872. The heavy buttresses either side of the porch suggest that rebuilding was fairly urgently required. This involved removing the gravestones by the porch to the right of the path. They were re-instated after the work was done - but in a different order!

Exton is a very pretty village with the River Meon flowing through it. (see right)

R.H.C. Ubsdell, Exton St. Peter and St. Paul Aug 1841
(PMRS 1945/419/18)

Exton St. Peter and St. Paul

Warnford CHURCH OF OUR LADY

R.H.C. Ubsdell, Warnford, Church of Our Lady 1841
(The Dean and Chapter of Winchester Cathedral)

R.H.C. Ubsdell, Warnford,
Church of Our Lady Aug 1841
(PMRS 1945/419/64)

Warnford Church sits in parkland landscaped by Capability Brown around 1760. The road in front of it was once the original Meon Valley road. This was however rebuilt in its current position and the village close to the church moved to its present position. The roof collapsed around 1909 and was rebuilt with the steeper pitch you see today. There is a wonderful display of snowdrops in the churchyard and park every February.

Warnford Church of Our Lady and snowdrops

The tower at Warnford is Norman added to a small Saxon church with an apse (a semi-circular east end). The original church was then enlarged in all directions under a single roof, leaving the Norman tower unchanged. It therefore illustrates a period of history where the conquerors create symbols of their conquest, but assimilate and are assimilated by the conquered, the resulting new nation then creating its own identity.

The original Saxon church was 8th or 9th century, the Norman tower was added about 1130, and the original church widened by around 6 feet and extended in around 1190. Brickwork at the top of the tower results from a rebuilding in 1752. The circular bell openings in the tower are most unusual. The roof was entirely renewed in 1906.

Norman Tower 1130 a.d.

On either side of the altar are the Neale Monuments. The Neales were exchequer officials under Elizabeth I and James I. The one on the right is the more impressive and is to Sir Thomas Neale and his two wives. The nine children of the last wife are shown on the side of the monument, the last four carrying skulls to show that they died in infancy.

Adam de Pont held the Manor of Warnford from 1171 to 1213 and it was he who enlarged the original Saxon church. The St. John family married into the de Ponts and built the 13th century hall that stands behind the church, turned into a scenic ruin in the 18th century. The Neales created a house for themselves near the parking area to the front of the church, but this was demolished in 1956.

Font of Purbeck Stone 1130 a.d.

Monument to Sir Thomas Neale (1621) and his two wives

The new church was a project by the Rector, Archdeacon Bayley in his old age and was consecrated by Charles Richard Sumner, (1790-1874) Bishop of Winchester (1827-1869) on 5th May 1846. It was an early work by the eminent Victorian architect Sir George Gilbert Scott, aged 32. Scott was influenced by Pugin and was best known for his gothic revival buildings. Sir George Gilbert Scott's most famous buildings are The Albert Memorial (1864-76) and The Midland Hotel fronting St. Pancras Station (1865). Whilst we might regret the loss of the old church which dated back to Saxon times, the new church is magnificent, although somewhat sinister on a rainy day! The new church is faced in knapped flints, knapped by the women of the village. William & Henry Lewis were the builders of the new church and they also tackled the reconstruction at Exton in 1847.

If cycling the Meon Valley Trail in one direction West Meon is a good place to start, as the prevailing gradient is downhill. Walkers can fairly easily scramble up at most road over-bridges but leaving the trail with a bike for the non-athletic is less easy at overbridges after Droxford. Droxford is a good place for a rest and the old railway hotel now called 'The Hurdles' is recommended. In June 1944 Allied leaders including, Churchill, Eisenhower and de Gaulle met in a train carriage at Droxford station to discuss the imminent D-Day invasion.

R.H.C. Ubsdell, West Meon 1841
(PMRS 1945/419/38)

R.H.C. Ubsdell, beieved to be the chancel Arch at the now demolished church at West Meon, but attributed by Ubsdell to Warnford
(PMRS 1945/419/65)

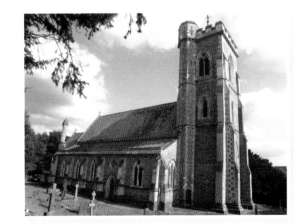

West Meon, St. John the Evangelist built 1846

Knapped Flints West Meon

East Meon ALL SAINTS

William Cobbett passed East Meon on one of his 'Rural Rides' and seeing the size of the church relative to the size of the surrounding population, used it to make the political point that the population must at one time have been much larger to build and support such a grand church. The rural population at the time Cobbett was writing was being displaced from the countryside to the towns by mechanisation of farming and the enclosure acts. However in respect of East Meon, at least, Cobbett was wrong. The church was built on such a huge scale between 1080 and 1150 by Bishop Walkelyn as a symbol of Norman dominance of the Saxon population, and the Bishops of Winchester who at this stage owned round a third of Hampshire, built their summer palace at Court House, now a private residence, just across the road. The only major change to Walkelyn's church came in 1230 when the south aisle and Lady Chapel were added. Henri de Blois, Bishop of Winchester, was grandson of William the Conqueror and brother of King Stephen. He imported seven black marble fonts into the country from Tournai in Belgium in 1150. There are examples in Winchester and Lincoln cathedrals and one here at

East Meon. The River Meon rises near East Meon and to the south lies Old Winchester Hill. Ubsdell is not known to have painted this church, but as East Meon would have dominated the Meon Valley for centuries it is difficult to write about the other churches of the Meon Valley without including it.

Winchester Hill

East Meon, All Saints

Hinton Ampner

*Hinton Ampner North Side
(National Trust, author)*

Ubsdell's churches are fascinating to visit, but Hinton Ampner is so close to West Meon and is such a delightful place to linger, that it is included here. Compared to some other properties there is little history here, for the Georgian core of the house, revealed after the demolition of Victorian additions in 1935, was itself rebuilt in 1960 following a fire, with much use of modern materials. Many of the contents had to be sourced from auctions and demolitions of other great houses, and the works of art, were to my mind, chosen more for decorative effect, than artistic or historical merit. As an example though of a mid-20th Century house built with no expense spared, it is absolutely fantastic. The mastermind behind the house was Ralph Dutton (1898-1985) who was to bequeath the 1650 acre estate that had been in the possession of the Stanwell & Dutton families for 400 years, to the National Trust in 1985.

It is however Ralph Dutton's gardens that are most superb, virtually every feature that you can incorporate in a garden is somewhere included:- terrace, pond, tree lined paths, dell, temple, walled garden, sunken garden, tennis court etc. The vistas are amazing, especially south, best seen from the bay window of Ralph Dutton's bedroom, and north where the tree lined paths lead you:- to the view over to the Civil War battleground of Cheriton.

*Hinton Ampner South Side
(National Trust, author)*

Waterlooville St. George's

R.H.C Ubsdell, Waterlooville St. George's 1841 (PMRS 1945/419/66)

Portsmouth, and later Southampton were vital to England for its defence and communications with the rest of the world. There were essentially two main routes to London from Portsmouth. Bearing in mind that it was easy to cross to Gosport, one route would be via the Meon Valley, Alton, and Farnham.

The main route however was along the west side of Portsea Island, Hilsea, climb the Portsdown Ridge at Cosham, Horndean, Waterlooville, Petersfield, Hindhead and The Devil's Punchbowl and Guildford.

Today there is a main route along the eastern side of Portsea Island and both crossings of the Ports Creek that divides the island from the mainland are swept east by the M27 to join the new A3(M) southern section of the London Road that joins the route of the original between Catherington and Blendworth. The most recent development has been the creation of a road tunnel underneath Hindhead that has removed that infamous bottleneck. To the east of the London Road and the London and

Overleaf: Isolated on the top of its hill, the beautiful church at Idsworth.

South Western Railway built it's direct line to London. The historic Stansted House is also not far away. The most stunning church in this area however is one Ubsdell did not paint, namely Idsworth.

The soldiers returning to Portsmouth on troopships from the battle of Waterloo (1815), after the first day's march from Portsmouth, set up camp at an unnamed hamlet of four dwellings and an ale house. The ale house was called 'The Heroes of Waterloo' after them, and the hamlet became known as firstly Waterloo, and then Waterlooville, to distinguish it from other settlements of the same name. Ubsdell painted two watercolours of the hamlet. The first illustrated the recently constructed 1829 St George's Church viewed from the 1711 Turnpike road to London, and the second seen over the head of a boy in a cornfield behind. The Turnpike had replaced the track between Horndean and Portsmouth which became impassable to coaches in the winter, making them divert via Havant. South of Catherington and Blendworth the A3 built on the old Turnpike route now diverts to the east to avoid the post war expansion of Waterlooville. The shopping precinct came in 1962 and The Wellington Arcade in 1965/6, next to the old church, which was itself replaced in 1970. Building of the Waterlooville Inner Relief Road allowed the shopping precinct along the old main road to be pedestrianised in 1985.

The Wellington Arcade and new church

R.H.C Ubsdell, St George's Church from the London Road 1841 (PMRS 1945/419/67)

Catherington All Saints

Catherington looks towards Hambledon and open countryside to the west but has sububan sprawl to north and south and the main London Road to the east.

Externally the church today is very similar to Ubsdell's watercolour of 1841 but the buttress, the dormer window and the sagging roof indicate the necessity for the 1883 restoration. In the North chapel there is a fine canopied tomb of Sir Nicholas Hyde and his wife with ten children represented on the front. Sir Nicholas was Chief Justice of England in the reign of Charles I.

R.H.C Ubsdell, Catherington, All Saints 1841
(PMRS 1945/419/9)

Blendworth St. Giles

Blendworth lies just to the East of the main London Road. The church that Ubsdell painted was Blendworth St Giles which lay in the Hamlet to the East of the present church. There had been a church on the site since the 14th Century but it was rebuilt in 1759. The church was declared unsafe in 1960 and demolished. The churchyard however remains.

The replacement church was Holy Trinity built 1851-2 designed by W.G. & E. Habershon.

Chalton, Blendworth, and Idsworth form part of the same Benefice. This beautiful chapel of 12th Century origin lay disused through much of the Victorian age and so escaped restoration until sensitive works by H.S. Goodhart-Rendel in 1912. Idsworth was not painted by Ubsdell.

*R.H.C Ubsdell, Blendworth, St. Giles, 1841
(PMRS 1945/419/5)*

Churchyard of the 14th Century Church

Blendworth, Holy Trinity

Hambledon ST. PETER & ST. PAUL

Hambledon lies in a Y shaped valley created by surrounding hills. The hills to west and east are covered with trees, Madam's & Boarhuts Copses to the west and 'The Hangers' to the east. A vineyard occupies some of the northern hill. The hills isolate Hambledon from the sprawl of Denmead, Horndean and modern-day Waterlooville to the southeast but wonderful open countryside lies towards the other points of the compass.

The heart of Hambledon is the High Street which runs for a short distance northwards from the main thoroughfare before passing round the east of the church to become Hogs Lane. Logically the main thoroughfare is called West Street on one side of the High Street, and East Street on the other. High Street with the old vicarage, church and churchyard at its head, and the village store on the other side of the street at the bottom, has the feel of a traditional village square.

Hambledon is famous for its cricket club founded about 1750 and which originally played on Broad-Halfpenny Down about 1½ miles away from the village on the road to Clanfield, under the guidance of Richard Nyren, landlord of the adjacent Bat & Ball Inn. The club left Broad-Halfpenny Down in 1782 as Richard was then landlord of the George Hotel in the village. The new cricket ground was just half a mile away on the road to Chidden. The Broadhalfpenny Brigands Cricket Club now play on the original site which is owned by Winchester College. Hambledon are credited with regulating the width of a cricket bat at 4¼ inches in 1771 and the weight of a cricket ball. The then president of the Hambledon club, the Earl of Winchilsea was a co-founder of the Mary-le-Bone Cricket Club (The MCC) in 1787, and Hambledon participated in the revision of the laws of cricket formulated in the following year.

Broadhalfpenny Brigands Cricket Club

High Street

Bat & Ball Inn

Richard Ubsdell's main competitor in Portsmouth was Richard Poate a fellow miniaturist. Poate had painted Hambledon Church in 1835. Ubsdell's version came 6 years later in 1841 and my photograph in 2010. The tower, south porch, and two storey vestry contained within them date from the 15th Century. The tower suffered a fire in 1794 and had been largely rebuilt. The treatment of the top of the tower seems to have changed between the Poate and Ubsdell version, as also the detailing around the arch of the external porch door. Big yews dominate the churchyard, the yew by the porch is remarkably similar in all three views, and a big yew in the artists' chosen viewpoints prevents the same positions being used today for the photograph.

The two 13th Century extensions eastwards can clearly be seen. The core of the original church is Saxon and north and south aisles were later added and extended. In all three pictures it can be seen that the main roof is tiled, but that the south aisle is lead covered. A major reconstruction and refurbishment took place in 1876. Accomodation in the roofspace in front of the tower was probably removed at that time.

Richard Poate. Hambledon St. Peter and St. Paul 1835
(The Dean and Chapter of Winchester Cathedral)

R.H.C Ubsdell, Hambledon, St. Peter and St. Paul 1841
(PMRS 1945/419/28)

Chalton St. Michael

Chalton as a village is beautifully situated and tranquil, a sufficient distance away to the east of the main London Road. It is just south of the Queen Elizabeth Country Park a mecca for walkers, mountain bikers, and horse riders. Just to the east lies the direct railway line to Portsmouth which threads its way along the valleys that lie between the downs. Beyond the railway is Compton Down and the National Trust Uppark Estate. The Sussex Border Path goes through the village and the Staunton Way passes to one side of the church. Food & drink are available at the picturesque thatched Red Lion pub which has a modern extension and large terrace to the rear overlooking the countryside.

The Red Lion, Chalton

The Staunton Way passes by the church

The church of Chalton, St Michael dates from the 13th Century. It is part of the same Benefice as Blendworth, Holy Trinity and Idsworth St. Hubert's. Ubsdell's watercolour was completed on July 18 1841. The chancel is slightly narrower than the nave and this is reflected in the different rooflines today, although Ubsdell's watercolour suggests that the rooflines were originally continuous. Ubdell's picture shows the large 15th Century north porch, some of whose timbers were incorporated in its smaller Victorian replacement. There is a monument set into the north wall of the chancel in memory of Richard Ball, its Rector who died in 1632. He is seen kneeling at a desk in the gown of a Bachelor of Divinity at Oxford. His coat of arms are displayed above a canopy supported by two Corinthian columns.

Chalton, St. Michael

R.H.C Ubsdell, Chalton, St. Michael 1841
(PMRS 1945/419/10)

Chalton, St. Michael interior

Clanfield St. Stephen

Clanfield marks the Northern limit of Portsmouth's sprawl. Ubsdell's watercolour of 1841 shows the 14th Century Church. The present church was designed in 1875 by R.J. Jones of Ryde. The church suffered arson in December 2007 which left just the walls standing, the interior and roof therefore now date from this 21st Century rebuilding.

Clanfield, St. Stephen

R.H.C Ubsdell, Clanfield, St. Stephen 1841
(PMRS 1945/419/12)

Uppark - Ubsdell's Victorian Afternoon

Sir Harry Fetherstonhaugh (22nd Dec 1754 to 24th Oct 1846) married his dairy maid, Mary Ann Bullock (1805-1874) in the Saloon at Uppark on 12th Sep 1825. She thus became Lady Fetherstonhaugh. She was 20, Sir Harry was 71, and would live to be 90. Sir Harry was a dissolute only-son who entertained the Prince Regent in 1784-5 by racing the Prince's jockey across the downs, and winning! It was Sir Harry who hired the 15 year old Emy Lyon, the future Lady Hamilton, out of prostitution in 1780 so that she could dance naked on the tables at Uppark for the entertainment of his houseparties. He would conceive a child with her, before passing her on at the age of 16 to Charles Greville, second son of the Earl of Warwick. Sir Harry owned Uppark, re-built around 1690 by the treacherous 1st Viscount Glendale, Earl of Tankerville. Lady Fetherstonhaugh would nurse him through old age, then see him buried in the Tankerville tomb in Harting Church. She would then run the estate she inherited, keeping up its traditions for a further 18 years.

Growing old with Mary Ann was her sister Frances Bullock (1818-1895) who would inherit the estate after her, and being childless, would then decide which children of their Sussex acquaintances should inherit it afterwards. Also growing old was Miss Sutherland (1806-1893) a love child of Sir Harry, and their housekeeper Sarah Wells. Sarah had been a lady's maid, but left in 1853 to marry Joseph Wells and have a son, the novelist H.G. Wells. She left her husband in 1880 and returned to be the housekeeper at Uppark until 1892.

Repton's additions to Uppark. The Dairy and its canopy on the far left where Sir Harry, so the story goes was enchanted by Mary Ann Bullock's singing, and to the right the stable block.

These old ladies lived in what has been characterised in the book *Uppark and its People* as a 'Victorian Afternoon'. It was Ubsdell's 'Victorian Afternoon' as well.

Ubsdell had run an amateur photographic club in Portsmouth in the 1850s and had been the first of its members to see the commercial possibilities of this new technology. With photography initially needing strong daylight Ubsdell began by producing libraries of stereoscopic images of famous landmarks. Then as techniques improved and less light was needed he saw the possibilities of photographic portraits, and the boom in photographic visiting cards:- the carte-de-visite. With his two sons working with him at 'Ubsdell Studio' he stole a march over his would-be photographic competitors and moved in 1859 to George Cole's old house at 1 Green Row, probably the best house in Old Portsmouth. It had two huge front rooms that would serve as studio and art gallery. The corner block had a first floor bay window that would serve as an 'abat-jour' letting in a huge amount of natural light into the photographic studio below.

The wealthy would of course summon a photographer to them, and so it was that in the early 1860s Ubsdell came to Uppark to take the photograph of Lady Fetherstonhaugh that appears in the guidebook of this National Trust property. She stands on the pebble path, edged by the back-bone knuckles of deer that leads to the game larder. It is an early photograph, for she stands rigid, her right hand holding an umbrella, her left hand resting on the back of an iron chair.

Ubsdell's contribution to Uppark can be found in the Flower Room which is off the Tapestry Room, where Sir Harry was nursed in his final years. On one wall is the picture of Vandalia his father's gothic folly. It celebrates Sir Matthew's investment in Iroquois Indian lands in the Ohio Valley near Pittsburg USA and stands on high land to the north of the house with views over to Sussex, Surrey and Hampshire and the Isle of Wight.

On the same wall is the picture dated 1862 of a gamekeeper standing by a pond with a pavilion set into the lake on its far side. This is probably the Engine House and pond at the bottom of the hill to Harting, close to the present Engine Farm. An early owner of Uppark, Sir Edward Ford (1605-70) is credited with inventing a reciprocating water pump, driven from an eccentric rotating wheel that raised water from the Thames to the highest streets in the City of London. How many different solutions to

were returning via Portsmouth from their honeymoon at Osborne on the Isle of Wight. Ubsdell also recorded the event, and had the opportunity to present 4 watercolours recording the celebrations in Portsmouth a week earlier to mark the wedding.

Ubsdell was a local celebrity, he could teach painting and photography, had a wicked sense of humour, and could play the piano and organ. He probably made an excellent house guest.

Photographic self portrait for inclusion in the picture of the Engine House and Pond

R.H.C. Ubsdell, The Engine House and Pond at the bottom of Harting Hill, 1862. The figure in the foreground is Ubsdell (National Trust CMS _upp2364)

R.H.C. Ubsdell, A Stag Hunt on Compton Down, New Year's Day 1st January 1864

getting water to Uppark were tried over the years is hard to say, but the last version of the wheel and pipes are in a brick building by the entrance to the farm at the bottom of the hill.

Ubsdell increased his fame in March 1863 by being selected by Portsmouth Corporation to produce a scroll to be presented to the newly married Edward and Alexandra, the Prince & Princess of Wales, who

In appreciation of his invitations to Uppark he produced watercolours and presented them to Lady Fetherstonhaugh. The first was 'Compton Down' which records the scene just south of Uppark, and is inscribed on the reverse with a label on its backboard 'Remembrance of a Snow Scene, Compton Down near Harting, Sussex 1st January 1864'. This was followed by 'Fishing Harting Pond' painted in Nov 1865.

R.H.C. Ubsdell, Fishing Harting Pond Nov 1865 (Stacey Gardner)

Harting Pond Today

Perhaps he sought comfort with Frances Bullock at Uppark. Above the door of the Butler's Pantry there is another of his works, 'Illuminations of H.M. The Queen's Fleet at Spithead August 13th 1878' on the back it is inscribed:-

'Presented to Miss Fetherstonhaugh as a tribute of gratitude'.

Hand Tinted Daylight Enlargement of a photograph of Lady Fetherstonhaugh 1874 presented to Frances Bullock in Remembrance of her Sister. (National Trust CMS_upp2569)

The Flower Room contains another remarkable picture presented to Frances Bullock in 1874, in remembrance of her sister. It is a daylight enlargement of Ubsdell's earlier photograph of Lady Fetherstonhaugh but beautifully stippled in watercolour using the techniques of a miniature painter to bring out the complexion of the face, and the shimmer of the satin and silk of the dress. Ubsdell was a Portsmouth Councillor from 1870 to 1874 and a member of the Portsmouth Sanitary Authority. The backboard of this painting is pasted to its frame with old minutes of this organisation that would eventually bring a working sewer system to the streets of Portsmouth.

Ubsdell's wife Mary Ann Pennal died of typhoid on the 6th April 1876, and his son William George, of heart disease age 40 on the 2nd Nov of the same year.

The autumn of Ubsdell's life saw more tragedy. His other sons were to die before him and he had to cope with a long illness and cancer of the tongue. He died at his grand-daughter's house at 57 Brompton Road, Landport on 4th June 1887 and is buried in an unmarked, re-used grave at Highland Road cemetery.

The Recreated Paintings

Queen Victoria's Visit to Portsmouth
March 21st 1842

Many of Ubsdell's portraits and historical scenes were in the Portsmouth Guildhall and Museum in the High Street when these buildings were destroyed by German bombing in World War II. These included his picture of Queen Victoria's visit to Portsmouth on March 21st 1842 (see page 26) and his picture of The Corporation of Portsmouth presenting his celebratory scrolls to Prince Edward & Princess Alexandra on board HMY Fairy following their honeymoon at Osborne in March 1863 (see page 43). Grainy black and white images of the pictures did however exist in the Annals of Portsmouth Corporation.

Portrait Artist Katie Chappell has managed to recreate the 1863 painting and the major personalities in the 1842 picture using the grainy photographs, the images in 'Sermon at St. Lawrence' (see page 88) and additional historical references.

The Corporation of Portsmouth present celebratory scrolls to Prince Edward and Princess Alexandra March 1863. Fort Blockhouse at the entrance to Portsmouth Harbour fires a Royal Salute in the background.

Acknowledgments, Bibliography & Reference

Between 1840 and 1846 Ubsdell walked the length and breadth of Hampshire calling at the big houses and estates, looking for portraiture work, as he passed through the towns and villages he painted watercolours of the local churches. This formed the basis for a very successful career ending in personal tragedy.

I have to extend my sincere thanks to all those who have helped me tell Ubsdell's story. Firstly I must thank Dr John Stedman of Portsmouth Museums and Records Service who produced from the vaults of Portsmouth Museums all their beautiful pictures for me to hold in my hands. His assistance went beyond that, persuading his colleagues to release copies of the images to me, and agreeing terms by which I could afford to reproduce them, and using them as the core of their wonderful Portraits and Landscapes exhibition to mark the Bicentenary of Ubsdell's birth. By a similar token I must thank Jo Bartholomew curator at Winchester Cathedral for allowing me similar access to the remarkable church watercolour collection of Bishop Charles Richard Sumner. Thanks also goes to Hampshire Records Office for allowing me to reproduce their images, and to David Rymill for reading my manuscript and offering many helpful suggestions. Many thanks also to distant cousin and Portsmouth resident Dave Quinton for similarly finding more of my errors.

This is a book about pictures and each page is in itself a picture. This is all the work of my talented designer Hannah Mee who drew on her years of experience with all the major publishers of children's books, and dealing with a legion of famous authors, some even more difficult then me!

Copyright is a major problem with a book such as this with so many previously unseen pictures, and I must thank organisations such as Portsmouth Museums, Winchester Cathedral, The Royal Collection, The National Maritime Museum, National Trust and English Heritage who were prepared to release their images on reasonable terms. I must also thank the private collectors and my distant cousins for releasing their images.

The beautiful coloured and fifth edition O.S. maps are out of copyright but the book owes a debt to their cartographers and David Archer Maps who supplied them. The text is culled from observation, conversations, and many hundreds of sources, and I thank the writers of the websites, church pamphlets, specialist books and information boards that have guided my comments, and crave their indulgence for my inclusion of snippets of their work in this overview.

The larger references are included in the bibliography. There are a great many more items I could have included, but I have included those items that affected me, and the text, the most.

The relevance of some items is indicated in brackets. My 'must read' references have an ® for 'recommended' against them.

This is an overview of Hampshire, of its historic people and places, and if it fails in academic rigour please forgive me, my aim was to produce something beautiful and accessible. I apologise for any errors and omissions. Please e-mail me with corrections and additional information, and I will update the next edition and website accordingly. Illustrations where the owners cannot be traced are marked (n.k.) I will be happy to acknowledgements their contributions in any future editions.

Thank you to Simon at Amiys Solutions for the design and development of the Ubsdell website.

Finally my thanks go to Jill my darling wife who has lived with me and my obsession for the past four years.

HAMPSHIRE BIBLIOGRAPHY

ON HAMPSHIRE

* A History of Hampshire And The Isle of Wight, The Victoria History of The Counties of England, Edited by William Page, 5 Volumes, Constable and Company Ltd. (collated known history of Hampshire by Manor, mostly digitised and available on-line)
* The Buildings of England, Hampshire and The Isle of Wight, Nikolaus Pevsner and David Lloyd, reprinted 2002 by Yale University Press ISBN 0 300 09606 2 (descriptions of virtually all significant buildings)
* Around Historic Hampshire, Colin Wintle, Drawings by Victor Spink, 1977, Midas Books, ISBN 0-85936-092 (descriptions of major villages and towns)
* A History of Hampshire, B. Carpenter Turner, 1963 ISBN 85033 254 0 (thematic history of Hampshire)

ON CHURCHES

* ® Historic English Churches, A guide to their Construction, Design and Features, Geoffrey R. Sharpe.
* Hampshire Churches, Margaret Green, Winton Publications, 1967 (Appendix has useful analysis of church features:- styles, towers, brasses, galleries, monuments, etc.)

GENERAL WALKING INFORMATION

* ® http://hampshire.walkandcycle.co.uk/trail_details.php?recordID=HAMPTR0044 O.S. based trail map
* ® www.hants.gov.uk/hampshiretreasures/ Hampshire C.C. database of notable Hampshire sites

18 ◦ PORTSMOUTH & THE STORY OF THE WATERCOLOURS

* ® A Portsmouth Canvas, The Art of the City and the Sea 1770-1970, Nigel Surry, The Fortune Press, 2008, ISBN 978-0-9559118-0-4
* ® Sir Frederic Madden and Portsmouth, John Webb, 1987, The Portsmouth Papers, Portsmouth City Council
* ® Thomas Ellis Owen, Shaper of Portsmouth, 'Father of Southsea', 2010, Sue Pike, Tricorn Books, ISBN 978-0-9562498-6-9 (church architect, collaborator with Ubsdell on some of the church watercolours)
* ® The Infernal Diver, John Bevan, 1996, (The story of John & Charles Deane, their invention of the diving helmet, and their recoveries from wrecks that Ubsdell recorded)
* Lord Bishop, The Life of Samuel Wilberforce 1805-1873, Standish Meacham, Harvard University Press, 1970 ISBN 674-53913-3
* The Royal Yacht Squadron Memorials of its Members, with an Enquiry into the History of Yachting and its Development in the Solent; and a Complete List of Members with their Yachts from the Foundation of the Club to the Present Time from the Official Records, Montague Guest and William B. Boulton, John Murray, 1903
* ® King Leopold's Ghost A Story of Greed, Terror and Heroism in Colonial Africa, Adam Hochschild, 2000 Pan Macmillan ISBN 978-0-330-44198-8 (Career of Major General Sir Francis Walter de Winton)
* Sir Francis De Winton, Administrateur Général du Congo 1884-1886, Marcel Luwel, Conservateur au Musée Royal de l'Afrique Centrale, Tervuren
* Home of the Fleet, A Century of Portsmouth Royal Dockyard in Photographs', Stephen Courtney & Brian Patterson, The History Press, 2009 ISBN 978 0 7524 4942 5
* Portsmouth, In Defence of the Realm, John Sadden, 2001, Phillimore, ISBN 1 86077 165 3
* Franz Xaver Winterhalter (1805-1873) Der Fürstenmaler Europas, Ingeborg Eismann, Michael Imhof Verlag
* Portsmouth The Old Town, Peter N. Rogers, 2008, Halsgrove, ISBN 978 1 84114 562 4

* ® Captain Marryat, Seaman, Writer and Adventurer. Tom Pocock, Stackpole Books, ISBN 0-8117-0355-X
* www.sewellgenealogy.com/p32.htm" \l "i436 for picture and bio of Major General Roger Stewart Beatson (Boathouse No. 6)

50 ◦ GOSPORT PENINSULA
GOSPORT PENINSULA
* The Story of Gosport, L.F.W. White 1964

76 ◦ ISLE OF WIGHT
http://studymore.org.uk/6bioh.htm"http://studymore.org.uk/6bioh.htm, Francis Thornhill, (Baring & Ward)
www.northwoodhouse.org/history.htm"http://www.northwoodhouse.org/history.htm (Northwood House)

88 ◦ PORTSDOWN RIDGE & COASTAL
SEAWARD SIDE
* The Nelson Monument Portsdown Hill, A Seamark Re-Discovered, Jane Smith, MA, Portsmouth Water Ltd, The Nelson Society 2007

102 ◦ MEON VALLEY
THE MEON VALLEY
* ® Villages of the Meon Valley Aspects of their History, Peter R. Watkins, Swanmore Books, ISBN 978-0-954-1566-3-3
* ® http://homepage.ntlworld.com/ron.strutt/rrcor3.html for history of the Meon Valley line and its remains
River Meon, Hillhead Harbour & Titchfield Haven
* The Noble Science: a few general ideas on fox-hunting, for the use of the rising generation of sportsmen, Frederick Peter Delmé Radcliffe, George Routledge, 1875

156 ◦ UPPARK – UBSDELL'S VICTORIAN AFTERNOON
* ® England's Mistress, The Infamous Life of Emma Hamilton, Kate Williams, 2007, Arrow Books, ISBN 9780099451839
* Uppark and its People, Margaret Meade-Fetherstonhaugh and Oliver Warner, Private Reprint 1971
* Uppark Guide Revised 2006, National Trust, (in particular the photograph of Mary Ann Fetherstonhaugh on page 31 and Frances Bullock page 32)
* Uppark Restored, Christopher Rowell and John Martin Robinson, National Trust 1996, ISBN 0 7078 0213 X